LIFE WITHOUT LIMIT

BOLA AKIN-JOHN

THY KINGDOM COME

Present And Future Manifestation Is For You And In You

Copyright (c) 2015 Dr. Francis Bola Akin-John

All rights reserved. No part may be reproduced without the written permission of the publisher.

ISBN: 978-978-941-438-3

All Scripture quotations are from King James Version of the Bible, unless otherwise stated.

Published by:

CHURCH GROWTH SERVICES INC.
Block C, FHA Abesan IV Estate, CF Street, Off CA Street, Mosan B/Stop, Ipaja, Lagos.
Tel: 08023000714, 08029744296, 08067301338
E-mail: akingrow@yahoo.com
website: www.icgm.com.ng www.bolaakinjohn.com

CONTENTS

Dedication	5
Appreciation	7
Introduction: Jesus and Political Power	9
1. Kingdom Defined	17
2. The Kingdom: Present and Future	25
3. The King Over the Kingdom	29
4. Citizens of the Kingdom	35
5. Kingdom of God Vs Kingdom of Satan	41
6. Personal Empire Vs Kingdom of God	47
7. The Kingdom of God and Idolatry Today	51
8. Kingdom Warfare	61
9. The Church and The Kingdom	69
10. Gospel of The Kingdom	75
11. Kingdom Praying	83
12. Kingdom Power	91
13. Kingdom Authority and Power	99
14. Kingdom Purpose and Principle	105
15. Kingdom Lifestyle	111
16. Kingdom Growth	117

17. Kingdom Mandate	125
18. Kingdom Ministries	131
19. Kingdom Harvest	137
20. Kingdom Leaders	145
21. Kingdom Finance	151
22. Kingdom Family	159
23. Kingdom-Driven Minister	163
24. Kingdom Glory	169

DEDICATION

This book is specially dedicated to the
**Founder, Foundation and
Head of the Kingdom**
- God the Father, Son and the Holy Spirit.

And those who are genuinely seeking,
building and extending the frontiers of His Kingdom
into every nook and corner of the earth.

LIFE WITHOUT LIMIT

APPRECIATION

Quite unlike my previous books, this one has taken me about 14 years before I started writing. Though I have thought on the subject severally in our Church Growth Institute but the burden to write the book became heavy on me few months ago and I thank God that eventually enabled me to pen it on paper in the space of four months, both home and abroad.

I thank the Lord that calls me into Kingdom ministry and made me to realize that there is a lot of difference between church and kingdom ministry.

I appreciate all my co-workers in the ministry who have cooperated and joined hands with me to build His Kingdom.

My printer is equally appreciated for his committed and competent service to His Kingdom.

APPRECIATION

My earnest prayer is for the kingdom of God to come into every heart reading this book and to all the world.

Introduction

JESUS AND POLITICAL POWER

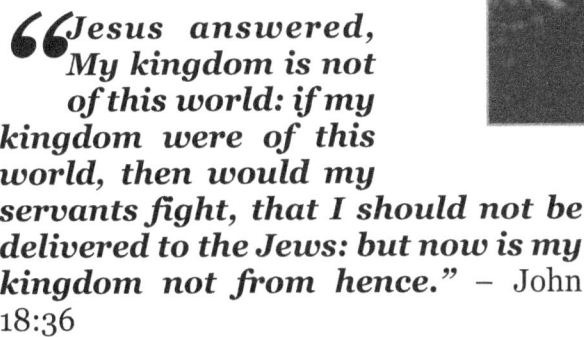

"*Jesus answered, My kingdom is not of this world: if my kingdom were of this world, then would my servants fight, that I should not be delivered to the Jews: but now is my kingdom not from hence.*" – John 18:36

"*Until the day in which he was taken up, after that he through the Holy Ghost had given commandments unto the apostles whom he had chosen: To whom also he shewed himself alive after his passion by many infallible proofs, being seen of them forty days, and speaking of the things pertaining to the kingdom of God: And, being assembled together with them, commanded them that they should not depart from*

INTRODUCTION

> *Jerusalem, but wait for the promise of the Father, which, saith he, ye have heard of me. For John truly baptized with water; but ye shall be baptized with the Holy Ghost not many days hence. When they therefore were come together, they asked of him, saying, Lord, wilt thou at this time restore again the kingdom to Israel? And he said unto them, It is not for you to know the times or the seasons, which the Father hath put in his own power. But ye shall receive power, after that the Holy Ghost is come upon you: and ye shall be witnesses unto me both in Jerusalem, and in all Judaea, and in Samaria, and unto the uttermost part of the earth."* – Acts 1:2-8

Even though the subject of the Kingdom of God is one of the course I have been teaching in our Post Graduate Diploma in Church Growth class in the last several years, yet the Lord has always burdened my heart to write a book on it in an elaborate way, so that many more people can have access to this most important mission of Jesus and basic foundation of our Christian faith.

The doctrine of the kingdom of God is the heart of the earthly ministry of our Lord Jesus. He introduced it, emphasized it, preached and taught it, lived it and demonstrated it for all to see. He commissioned His

INTRODUCTION

disciples to go and preach the gospel of the kingdom.

> *"The Spirit of the Lord is upon me, because he hath anointed me to preach the gospel to the poor; he hath sent me to heal the brokenhearted, to preach deliverance to the captives, and recovering of sight to the blind, to set at liberty them that are bruised,"* – Luke 4:18

> *"From that time Jesus began to preach, and to say, Repent: for the kingdom of heaven is at hand."* – Matthew 4:17

And He declared unequivocally that **"My kingdom is not of this world"** (John 18:36)

Yet the right understanding of the Kingdom initially eluded the disciples, that was why they were asking questions about political power at the ascension of Jesus (Acts 1:2-8) Jesus was talking about the Kingdom and the disciples were asking questions about political power. The same dilemma we see largely in the church of today.

Too many church leaders are doing ministry without proper knowledge of the Kingdom of God and they only understand it in the context of political power. The more reason church leaders are canvassing for political power so as to better their nations.

INTRODUCTION

There have been lots of erroneous teachings that emphasize that Christians must seize political power, become Presidents, Governors, Senators, and top government functionaries so as to lead the nation in Christian ways. It is as if politics and political positions, not Jesus are the answer to the problems of our nation.

While a nation can be influenced with kingdom principles if those at the helm of affairs are true citizens of His kingdom and they are living the kingdom lifestyle, yet the emphasis of Jesus remains that 'my kingdom is not of this world', meaning that He came only to establish and spread His spiritual kingdom in the heart of men, and not to seize political power or rule the worldly kingdom.

A gang of thieves broke into a jewelry's store one night. Instead of stealing, they were on a different mission – they changed the price tags of all the items. The following morning, people came and exchanged millions of money for worthless items and paid little for precious items because the thieves were careful and nobody noticed.

So also today, kingdom values have been changed and lots of Christians are spending their lives buying worthless things of this life and forgetting those things of eternal values of the kingdom.

The study of the scripture has shown that the kingdom of God was the central mission and message of Jesus. To miss the significance of the kingdom in the gospels is to fail to understand the life, work and teaching of Christ. His ministry was the ministry of the kingdom; His teaching showed men and women how to enter it; His works proved it had come; His parables taught it's mysteries and His prayers taught the disciples to desire its full expression.

Jesus made it clear that the struggle in which He was engaged was a battle between the kingdom of God and the kingdom of darkness. He came to invade this present evil age with the powers of the age to come and He did it in the lives of men and women by attacking the works of the enemy. Jesus' words and works demonstrated the presence of the rule of God on earth. In Jesus, the future has broken into the present.

Jesus did not come for political power but to establish His spiritual kingdom in the world. He is a spiritual king than a politician. It is this knowledge that this book aims to disseminate to the body of Christ. The message and gospel of the kingdom is very scarce in our pulpits today and the devil is happy about it. The more reason the church is floundering and true disciples are hard to come by in our society.

Until every believer and church leader is soundly knowledgeable about the kingdom, many things will keep on going wrong in our lives and the church will become a laughing stock in our world. We must know that the kingdom has come and is still coming. The kingdom is relevant today and will be for all eternity. Our heart cry everyday must be, LORD, let your kingdom come into our hearts, communities, nations and churches.

> *"After this manner therefore pray ye: Our Father which art in heaven, Hallowed be thy name. Thy kingdom come. Thy will be done in earth, as it is in heaven."* – Matthew 6:9-10

Dr. Francis Bola Akin-John
Lagos - Nigeria
December, 2014

INTRODUCTION

This song captures it all:

Thy kingdom come o God
Thy rule o Christ begin
Break with thine iron rod
The tyrannies of sin.

Where is thy reign of peace?
And purity and love
When shall hatred cease
As in the realm above.

Men are despising your name
Wolves are devouring your flock
Much shameful behaviours
Shows that love is cold.

When comes the promised time
That war shall be no more
And just, oppression, curse
Shall flee thy face before.

Darkness hovers there still
In Gentile land near and far
Arise thou the morning star
Arise, and set no more.

We pray the Lord arise
And come in thy great power
Revive our longing eyes
Which languish for thy sight.

CHAPTER ONE

Chapter One
KINGDOM DEFINED

O ur Lord Jesus made a profound statement to the religious leaders of His days in Matthew 22:29;

> *"Jesus answered and said unto them, ye do err, not knowing the scriptures, nor the power of God".*

That is the most heinous position to be in the church – being ignorant of the truth of God's word. When one is in such stage, he or she will surely err, go wrong and lead people astray.

This is the condition that many Christians and ministers have found themselves today concerning the subject of the kingdom of God. So many of us have read the gospels several times but have not come to proper grasp and understanding of the Kingdom, as our Lord Jesus meant it. Our lack of proper understanding of it has created much confusion in our prayers, outreaches, lifestyles and

CHAPTER ONE

general perception of the operations of God in this world. Generally speaking, there are three misconceptions about the kingdom of God over the years:

Firstly, the Jews expected that the first coming of Jesus was meant to bring the kingdom back to Israel; to destroy their enemies, dislodge the Romans and become their political ruler.

> *"And I will bring again the captivity of my people of Israel, and they shall build the waste cities, and inhabit them; and they shall plant vineyards, and drink the wine thereof; they shall also make gardens, and eat the fruit of them." –*
> Amos 9:14

> *"Thus saith the LORD of hosts; There shall yet old men and old women dwell in the streets of Jerusalem, and every man with his staff in his hand for very age. And the streets of the city shall be full of boys and girls playing in the streets thereof. Thus saith the LORD of hosts; If it be marvellous in the eyes of the remnant of this people in these days, should it also be marvellous in mine eyes? saith the LORD of hosts. Thus saith the LORD of hosts; Behold, I will save my people from the east country, and from the west country; And I will bring them, and they shall*

> *dwell in the midst of Jerusalem: and they shall be my people, and I will be their God, in truth and in righteousness."* – Zechariah 8:4-8

Jesus becoming a king?

> *"Then those men, when they had seen the miracle that Jesus did, said, This is of a truth that prophet that should come into the world. When Jesus therefore perceived that they would come and take him by force, to make him a king, he departed again into a mountain himself alone."* – John 6:14-15

Many are still in this delusion today that Jesus is only for the Jews. Great misconceptions!

Secondly, there is the misconception that the kingdom is only futuristic. It is believed that the kingdom will be in heaven and we cannot attain or know the kingdom now.

> *"And in the days of these kings shall the God of heaven set up a kingdom, which shall never be destroyed: and the kingdom shall not be left to other people, but it shall break in pieces and consume all these kingdoms, and it shall stand for ever. Forasmuch as thou sawest that the stone was cut out of the mountain without hands, and that it brake in*

> *pieces the iron, the brass, the clay, the silver, and the gold; the great God hath made known to the king what shall come to pass hereafter: and the dream is certain, and the interpretation thereof sure."* - Daniel 2:44-45.

People with this perception believe that only few people can get to and enjoy the kingdom of God when it will eventually come.

Thirdly, there is the misconception that the kingdom will come during the second coming of Christ at the millennium reign on earth. That is the one thousand years (1,000 years) literal reign of Christ in bliss on the earth in distant future.

> *"Strengthen ye the weak hands, and confirm the feeble knees. Say to them that are of a fearful heart, Be strong, fear not: behold, your God will come with vengeance, even God with a recompence; he will come and save you. Then the eyes of the blind shall be opened, and the ears of the deaf shall be unstopped. Then shall the lame man leap as an hart, and the tongue of the dumb sing: for in the wilderness shall waters break out, and streams in the desert."* - Isaiah 35:3-6

During that time, there would be no more wars and peace would reign on the earth.

The truth however is that the kingdom of God is much more than all these; while there are elements of truth in these misconceptions, yet they are not the whole truth about the kingdom of God as Jesus taught and practiced it during His earthly ministry.

Kingdom Meaning

The world's mindset conceives of kingdoms largely in terms of geographical area over which a sovereign king exercises authority, but the Biblical term implies reign and rule. Kingdom is translated from the New Testament Greek word, 'basileia' – meaning an exercise of kingly rule and reign rather than simply establishing a geographical area over which a king rules.

The kingdom of God is the dynamic and spiritual rule and reign of God in the hearts and lives of men and women. It is not a political reign or physical kingdom territories, but making changes in the spiritual order in the lives of men and women. The kingdom of God co-exists with human sovereignties, but majorly changing men and women from within.

The kingdom is the coming of Christ into the world to assert His power, glory and rights against the kingdom of darkness, dominion of sin and course of this present world. It is more than salvation from sin or the church; it is God expressing Himself with power and ruling in the hearts and lives of men and women in the world.

CHAPTER ONE

> *"Jesus answered and said unto him, If a man love me, he will keep my words: and my Father will love him, and we will come unto him, and make our abode with him."* – John 14:23

> *"And when he had said this, he breathed on them, and saith unto them, Receive ye the Holy Ghost:"* – John 20:22

The kingdom is now present in the world with power. Jesus declared the manifesto of the kingdom in Luke chapter 4 verses 18 and 19. This kingdom power is not political or material but spiritual. That is, the kingdom is not a religio-political theocracy; nor a matter of social or political dominion over the nations of this world. That is why we must all seek the kingdom first into our hearts and lives.

> *"But seek ye first the kingdom of God, and his righteousness; and all these things shall be added unto you."* - Matthew 6:33

The kingdom must be inside us and rule within everyone.

> *"And when he was demanded of the Pharisees, when the kingdom of God should come, he answered them and said, The kingdom of God cometh not with observation: Neither shall*

> *they say, Lo here! or, lo there! for, behold, the kingdom of God is within you."* - Luke 17:20-21

It is the kingdom within that must take charge of our environments. We must all pray the kingdom into our hearts.

> *"After this manner therefore pray ye: Our Father which art in heaven, Hallowed be thy name. Thy kingdom come. Thy will be done in earth, as it is in heaven."* - Matthew 6:9-10.

CHAPTER ONE

Chapter Two

THE KINGDOM: PRESENT AND FUTURE

Our Lord Jesus specifically taught that we should pray for the coming and manifestation of the kingdom of God here on earth (Matthew 6:9-10). Even though there is a future aspect to the kingdom of God, yet there is the immediate aspect of the manifestation of God's kingdom now.

Repeatedly, the terms "kingdom of God" and "kingdom of heaven" are used interchangeably in the scripture. While kingdom of heaven talks about the future aspect which is the second coming of Christ and eternal home of believers, kingdom of God talks about the immediate reign of Christ now in the world.

> *"From that time Jesus began to preach, and to say, Repent: for the kingdom of heaven is at hand."* - Matthew 4:17

CHAPTER TWO

> *"And saying, The time is fulfilled, and the kingdom of God is at hand: repent ye, and believe the gospel."* –
> Mark 1:15

In other instances, they both represent the same thing and meaning. The kingdom of heaven refers to the age to come, while the kingdom of God refers to this age we are living in. The two kingdoms span the timeline of human history, beginning with the fall of humanity in the Garden of Eden. When Jesus came to earth the first time, humanity entered the last days - the time period between Christ's resurrection and the second coming (eternity) at the end of the world. The two kingdoms overlap in time.

The age to come invades the present, pushing back the kingdom of darkness. The glimpse of eternity that came with Christ (the blind seeing, the dead risen, pain easing) continues today, but not perfectly. That's why we must understand that 'the kingdom is here, but not fully here'. There is a tension, caused by constant spiritual warfare. By faith, citizens of the kingdom live in the age to come, but Satan works to keep us in this Age. When Christ returns, this Age will end and we will experience the fullness of God's eternal kingdom of heaven.

We are awaiting its ultimate fulfillment, and this causes many people to struggle. The church lives "between the times" – between the inauguration and consummation of the kingdom, between the "already" and the "not yet". The Age to come has entered the present, and under this new rule, we can expect to receive the benefits of that Age: forgiveness of sin, freedom from demons, victorious living and healing from sickness, but not without a battle.

What's unique about the era in which we live is that although the enemy's power is curbed, he has not been rendered totally powerless. The church is being called as God's army to cooperate with the Holy Spirit, continually assault the citadels of Satan, and bring the rule of God to hearts, bodies and lives of men and women.

> *"But if I cast out devils by the Spirit of God, then the kingdom of God is come unto you."* - Matthew 12:28

The early church lived with the understanding that they were to continue Jesus' ministry on earth, ministering wholeness in an overall and inclusive sense. The church today cannot shrink from this responsibility too. While we are hoping and praying for the coming kingdom of heaven, yet we must manifest and demonstrate the kingdom of God here and now. We must be people of the kingdom and spread that kingdom to hearts and places far and beyond. The will of God must be done here on earth as it is done in heaven.

A very popular and highly placed Bishop and preacher was found dead on his bed one morning. His close Associates were aghast and surprised. One of them asked; 'where has he gone?' 'Heaven, of

CHAPTER TWO

course', replied the other. But his personal Assistant interjected by saying, "I have served him closely for more than 10 years. He always prepared for whatever he is going to do. If he wants to travel, he would prepare, pray, get ready and talk about it for weeks. But I never heard him talk or prepare for heaven, so I'm not sure he went there, because my Bishop never go on a journey he is not prepared for".

Chapter Three
THE KING OVER THE KINGDOM

Jesus Christ of Nazareth is the king over the spiritual kingdom of God. He announced that the kingdom of God had come in Him.

> *"But if I cast out devils by the Spirit of God, then the kingdom of God is come unto you."* - Matthew 12:28

He invaded this earth to destroy the kingdom of Satan and set everything right.

> *"He that committeth sin is of the devil; for the devil sinneth from the beginning. For this purpose the Son of God was manifested, that he might destroy the works of the devil."* - I John 3:8

> *"How God anointed Jesus of Nazareth with the Holy Ghost and with power: who went about doing good, and healing all that were*

> *oppressed of the devil; for God was with him."* - Acts 10:38

He is given authority and power by the Father.

> *"Now is the judgment of this world: now shall the prince of this world be cast out."* – John 12:31

> *"For the Father loveth the Son, and sheweth him all things that himself doeth: and he will shew him greater works than these, that ye may marvel. For as the Father raiseth up the dead, and quickeneth them; even so the Son quickeneth whom he will. For the Father judgeth no man, but hath committed all judgment unto the Son: That all men should honour the Son, even as they honour the Father. He that honoureth not the Son honoureth not the Father which hath sent him."* – John 5:20-23

Jesus is co-equal with God. He is the very Son of God and possesses the same attributes like the Father. He is the second Person in the Trinity – Father, Son and Holy Spirit. He left heaven with the permission of His Father to earth so as to live, and died as full man, full God and resurrected triumphantly over sin, Satan and the world, in order to set man free from the bondage of sin and Satan. He came to take back the spiritual authority that the first Adam sold into the hand of Satan. Where the first Adam failed, Jesus as the last Adam succeeded.

> *"For if by one man's offence death reigned by one; much more they which receive abundance of grace and of the gift of righteousness shall reign in life by one, Jesus Christ.) Therefore as by the offence of one judgment came upon all men to condemnation; even so by the righteousness of one the free gift came upon all men unto justification of life. For as by one man's disobedience many were made sinners, so by the obedience of one shall many be made righteous."*
> - Romans 5:17-19

Jesus as the king over the kingdom of God will rule and reign forever in power and authority.

> *"I saw in the night visions, and, behold, one like the Son of man came with the clouds of heaven, and came to the Ancient of days, and they brought him near before him. And there was given him dominion, and glory, and a kingdom, that all people, nations, and languages, should serve him: his dominion is an everlasting dominion, which shall not pass away, and his kingdom that which shall not be destroyed. These great beasts, which are four, are four kings, which shall arise out of the earth."* –

CHAPTER THREE

Daniel 7:13-14, 17.

He will reign until all enemies are subdued;

> *"Then cometh the end, when he shall have delivered up the kingdom to God, even the Father; when he shall have put down all rule and all authority and power. For he must reign, till he hath put all enemies under his feet."* – 1 Corinthians 15:24-25.

> *"The LORD said unto my Lord, Sit thou at my right hand, until I make thine enemies thy footstool. The LORD shall send the rod of thy strength out of Zion: rule thou in the midst of thine enemies."* – Psalm 110:1-2

He will overcome and prevail and then hand over everything into the hand of the Father;

> *"Then cometh the end, when he shall have delivered up the kingdom to God, even the Father; when he shall have put down all rule and all authority and power. For he must reign, till he hath put all enemies under his feet."* – 1 Corinthians 15:24-25.

Since His first coming and vicarious death on the

cross and triumphant resurrection (Colossians 2:15) Christ has set up His kingdom in the heart of men and women. He is the king of hearts. He takes residence in the hearts that are opened to Him and rule and reign there.

> *"Behold, I stand at the door, and knock: if any man hear my voice, and open the door, I will come in to him, and will sup with him, and he with me."* – Revelation 3:20

> *"To whom God would make known what is the riches of the glory of this mystery among the Gentiles; which is Christ in you, the hope of glory:"* - Colossians 1:27

He rules and reigns in the hearts of people across nations, languages, groups and kingdoms of men.

There is no way to have His kingdom in your heart and life if you don't submit to His Lordship over your life and hearts. He must be the king over your life and living. You must believe in Him and obey Him without question, if you are going to reign with Him here and hereafter. In spite of opposition from satanic kingdom and carnalities of men, Christ is the undisputed king of life and eternity. You may be religious but until you sincerely and genuinely welcome Him into your heart and crown Him the king there, you cannot be a citizen of His kingdom.

He will surely reign now and throughout eternity and will slay those who are His enemies.

Today, He is the Lamb on the throne, willing to save, heal and deliver. But in the kingdom of heaven, He will be the Lion that will kill, devour and destroy all His enemies.

There is no kingdom without a king and Jesus is the undisputed King of God's kingdom, both now and in eternity. To His kingship and Lordship we must all bow and obey! For He is the King of kings and Lord of lords.

Chapter Four
CITIZENS OF THE KINGDOM

Since the kingdom of God is a spiritual one, only those who are spiritually enlightened can be citizens of that kingdom.

> *"For they that are after the flesh do mind the things of the flesh; but they that are after the Spirit the things of the Spirit. For to be carnally minded is death; but to be spiritually minded is life and peace."* – Romans 8:5-6

It is possible to be a professed Christian and yet not be a citizen of His kingdom. Carnal, religious and nominal Christians are yet to be in His spiritual kingdom. There are too many religious and secular people in churches today who are yet to become citizens of His kingdom. Many of them have their names in the register of the church, but unfortunately their names are not written in the Lamb's book.

Everyone that commits sin is in the kingdom of Satan and is being dominated by the forces of evil in this world. It is only by genuine change of heart that can open the way to the kingdom of Christ.

The number one and only entrance into His kingdom is through genuine repentance.

> *"And saying, The time is fulfilled, and the kingdom of God is at hand: repent ye, and believe the gospel."* – Mark 1:15

> *"Jesus answered and said unto him, Verily, verily, I say unto thee, Except a man be born again, he cannot see the kingdom of God."* – John 3:3

True repentance leads to godly sorrow for sin and turning away from it and inviting Christ into your heart;

> *"Now I rejoice, not that ye were made sorry, but that ye sorrowed to repentance: for ye were made sorry after a godly manner, that ye might receive damage by us in nothing. For godly sorrow worketh repentance to salvation not to be repented of: but the sorrow of the world worketh death."* – 2 Corinthians 7:9-10

> *"For all those things hath mine hand made, and all those things have been, saith the LORD: but to this*

> *man will I look, even to him that is poor and of a contrite spirit, and trembleth at my word."* – Isaiah 66:2

Repentance grants you entrance into His kingdom within you. Genuine repentance automatically translates you from the kingdom of darkness into His glorious kingdom.

Furthermore, the fruits of repentance must show forth in your daily living. The inner change and transformation must show forth in your daily living, choices, words and actions. There will be a marked difference in your life and old things must pass away if truly you have entered His spiritual kingdom.

> *"Therefore if any man be in Christ, he is a new creature: old things are passed away; behold, all things are become new."* – 2 Corinthians 5:17

As a citizen of His kingdom, you must shine as light in the world and be a salt of the earth. Citizens of the kingdom must never live in sin, worldliness, disobedience and ungodliness; else they will be cast out.

> *"And I say unto you, That many shall come from the east and west, and shall sit down with Abraham, and Isaac, and Jacob, in the kingdom of heaven. But the children of the kingdom shall be cast out into outer darkness: there shall be*

weeping and gnashing of teeth." – Matthew 8:11-12.

Citizens of the kingdom will come from every tribe and tongue, and there will be no respect of persons, or favouritism. It is when you are living godly, obediently and righteously that you can remain as bonafide citizens of His kingdom.

> *"Therefore say I unto you, The kingdom of God shall be taken from you, and given to a nation bringing forth the fruits thereof. And whosoever shall fall on this stone shall be broken: but on whomsoever it shall fall, it will grind him to powder."* – Matthew 21:43-44.

For the kingdom of God is not about carnal, secular and material things, but righteousness, peace and joy in the Holy Spirit.

> *"For the kingdom of God is not meat and drink; but righteousness, and peace, and joy in the Holy Ghost."* – Romans 14:17.

It goes therefore that nations and worldly kingdoms may close doors against the church, but not against His rule in the hearts of people. Physical church buildings may not be permitted or allowed in certain places, yet, the kingdom of God is thriving and will continue to thrive. That is why the kingdom of God have survived Communism, Buddhism, Shintoism,

Mohammedalism and all the religious and secular 'Isms' over the centuries.

Kings and Priests

Citizens of the kingdom are made kings and priests by Christ. Jesus is the Senior King and every true believer is the junior king and priest in the kingdom.

> *"And from Jesus Christ, who is the faithful witness, and the first begotten of the dead, and the prince of the kings of the earth. Unto him that loved us, and washed us from our sins in his own blood, And hath made us kings and priests unto God and his Father; to him be glory and dominion for ever and ever. Amen."*
> – Revelation 1:5-6.

> *"And hast made us unto our God kings and priests: and we shall reign on the earth."* – Revelation 5:10.

As kings and priests, we must rule and reign over sin, Satan and corruptions of this present world by His power and authority. As kings we must overcome sin and temptations - rule over sicknesses, diseases and demonic onslaughts of the host of darkness. We must live victoriously and prevailingly over the works of the devil.

> *"Ye are of God, little children, and have overcome them: because*

greater is he that is in you, than he that is in the world." – John 4:4

"For whatsoever is born of God overcometh the world: and this is the victory that overcometh the world, even our faith. Who is he that overcometh the world, but he that believeth that Jesus is the Son of God?" – 1 John 5:4-5.

It is a spiritual kingdom and we must reign as spiritual kings with Christ. As priests, we must do service to God and bring people to Him. We must intercede and lead people in worship of Him and unto Him. As priests, we are to bring Him closer to the people and bring the people closer to Him. We are to expand and extend His kingdom into hearts and places, exert His authority and pull down the kingdom of darkness in our communities.

Chapter Five

KINGDOM OF GOD vs KINGDOM OF SATAN

Unseen, unknown and mysterious to many eyes is a spiritual world above and beyond this earthly sphere. Yet, that spiritual world is real and relevant to this our earthly sphere. Whatever happens in the earth is first determined in that spiritual world. The battle for this world is primarily a spiritual battle.

There is a cosmic world that rules the earthly world. The Cartoon World and Esoteric Films show these. The Witches of Endor, Narnia and Captain America Cartoons are proves of spiritual beings showing forces of good and evil contending for our world. These human creations are not figment of some people's imaginations only but a deep confirmation of what many failed to see and acknowledge.

In biblical terms, the spiritual battle for the world is between God and Satan. Jesus acknowledged that Satan has a kingdom and is the prince of this world.

CHAPTER FIVE

> *"And if Satan cast out Satan, he is divided against himself; how shall then his kingdom stand?"* – Matthew 12:26

> *"And the devil said unto him, All this power will I give thee, and the glory of them: for that is delivered unto me; and to whomsoever I will I give it. If thou therefore wilt worship me, all shall be thine."* – Luke 4:6-7.

The New Testament presents the world as estranged from God and seized by Satan.

> *"Now is the judgment of this world: now shall the prince of this world be cast out."* – John 12:31

> *"Hereafter I will not talk much with you: for the prince of this world cometh, and hath nothing in me."* – John 14:30

> *"But if our gospel be hid, it is hid to them that are lost: In whom the god of this world hath blinded the minds of them which believe not, lest the light of the glorious gospel of Christ, who is the image of God, should shine unto them."* – 2 Corinthians 4:3-4

Since Adam fell into sin in the Garden of Eden, Satan usurped that authority and became the de-facto ruler of the world. He set up his kingdom and became the ruler of darkness with his demons and agents. The kingdom of Satan is manifested by sin, wickedness, sicknesses, diseases, poverty, injustice, immoralities, murder, violence, wars, calamities, cheating, abortion, lies, idol worship, graven images, rituals, altars, cultism, effigies, sacred temples, human sacrifices and occultic practices.

Wherever these are in operations, the kingdom of evil, Satan, darkness and bondage are in mighty operations. Looking across the world today, you cannot but see that the physical manifestations of the kingdom of darkness are everywhere and in every place.

The Kingdom of God

The fundamental principle of the kingdom of God is the demonstration of God's power through Christ. The kingdom of God is primarily an assertion of divine power in action.

> *"For the kingdom of God is not in word, but in power."* – 1 Corinthians 4:20

When Jesus announced that the kingdom of God had come in Him, He claimed for Himself the position of a divine invader who came with a superior power to take back the usurped power of Satan. He entered this territory of Satan and took back the authority that he stole from Adam and gives it back to His kingdom citizen.

> *"But if I cast out devils by the Spirit of God, then the kingdom of God is come unto you. Or else how can one enter into a strong man's house, and spoil his goods, except he first bind the strong man? and then he will spoil his house."* – Matthew 12:28-29

> *"Behold, I give unto you power to tread on serpents and scorpions, and over all the power of the enemy: and nothing shall by any means hurt you. Notwithstanding in this rejoice not, that the spirits are subject unto you; but rather rejoice, because your names are written in heaven."*
> - Luke 10:19-20

Jesus demonstrated spiritual victory over the devil in the wilderness encounter (Matthew 4:11); spiritual power over the rule of Satan (Matthew 12:28); power to work miracles and heal the sick (Acts 4:30); casting out demons and deliverance to the oppressed (Luke 4:18-20; Mark 1:27); salvation and sanctification of those who believe the gospel (John 3:3; 17:17; Acts 2:38-40); the death and resurrection of Christ completed and consummated the victory of Christ over Satan and restored the power of the kingdom of God to every believer (John 12:23-32).

Today in every human affair, the kingdom of darkness is still ruling and reigning. Every believer has the responsibility and authority to demonstrate and bring the power of the kingdom of God to bear in every situation. We must demonstrate the victory of Christ over that of Satan firstly in our lives and in the life of others. We must bring the kingdom of God into the territories of our lives, churches and communities. It's a daily spiritual battle, but we are assured of victory in Christ.

> ***"And having spoiled principalities and powers, he made a shew of them openly, triumphing over them in it."***
> – Colossians 2:15

By kingdom power, we must preach the gospel of the kingdom and see people translated from the kingdom of darkness into the kingdom of light.

> ***"Who hath delivered us from the power of darkness, and hath translated us into the kingdom of his dear Son:"*** - Colossians 1:13

The kingdom of God is manifested in peace, joy, salvation from sin, sickness, diseases, Holy living, justice, righteous works, good news, and gospel power to change and covert people, growth, blessings and glories of the Lord.

Believers must therefore seek to bring the kingdom of God into the territories, hearts and places where the kingdom of darkness is still ruling and reigning. The victorics of Christ must be enforced in our world. The power of the kingdom must cancel and negate the manifestations of the kingdom of darkness everywhere.

Chapter Six

PERSONAL EMPIRE vs KINGDOM OF GOD

It is without gainsay to declare that many preachers and leaders are simply building their own empire rather than build the kingdom of God today. In these days of independent ministries, lots of people have risen up to build their own empires and shamelessly negate the truth and principles of His kingdom. I have seen, known and heard of preachers who gather crowds, build cathedrals but whose people don't show evidence of being truly born again Christians.

While the kingdom of God consists of getting people saved, transformed and discipled for Christ, and showing fruits of righteousness in their daily lives, personal empire is gathering people into a religious idea, message, emphasis and man-made ideologies that makes people more carnal than spiritual, secular than godly, worldly minded than heavenly minded and materially prosperous than spiritually prosperous in God.

These are the evidences in open display in many churches and ministries in the last 30 years. Preachers after preachers have stylishly built their own financial and ministerial empires through the avenue of the church.

Personal Empire In The Making

You start building your personal empire when you deviate from the whole truth of the Bible; join a club or group of ministers that do ministry with the motives of money; use your pulpit to preach secular issues; write books that have no scriptural quotations; air non-religious programmes and meetings; compromise the Bible truth so as to attract crowds; becoming friends with people at the helm of affairs in the government without speaking the truth of God's word to them and using the message of grace as a license to cover sins and gross sinful lifestyles.

It is on record that preachers that water down the gospel have become crowd pullers, gained so much financial blessings and build large empire of network of 'churches' and protégés in ministry. But the reality is that their empires will begin to crumble from within after few years and their churches will begin to nosedive. Because every empire of man will collapse, only the kingdom of God will endure.

Building His Kingdom

Every minister is called by God to build and extend His kingdom, not personal empire. The man that God uses must never be more important than the kingdom he represents. The King over the kingdom is whom every one of us must follow, worship and submit to. The Lordship of Christ must never be in question in our lives if we are going to build His kingdom. We must therefore use our gifts, privileges and opportunities to preach Jesus, talk Jesus, show Jesus to people and bring people to the kingdom of Jesus Christ.

Our churches and ministries must project kingdom principles and values more than anything else. We must never compromise the kingdom gospel for popular acceptance. Our stand, values and principle must be clear for all to see the message of Jesus and His kingdom must take preeminence over every other thing.

Compromising the scripture for financial gain and worldly pleasures will pay you initially, but will make God to be angry with your work and He will surely destroy the empire you have built, sooner or later. No human empire will ever compete with His eternal kingdom; they will all pale into eternal insignificance. Already, many personal kingdoms of men have collapsed and continue to collapse. Only His kingdom will last.

CHAPTER SIX

The pertinent question every gospel minister must answer is this; Am I building His kingdom or my personal empire with my ministry and ministrations?

Chapter Seven
THE KINGDOM OF GOD AND IDOLATRY TODAY

The system, cultures, values and beliefs of this world are opposed to God. The world system is controlled by the prince of this world.

> *"But if our gospel be hid, it is hid to them that are lost: In whom the god of this world hath blinded the minds of them which believe not, lest the light of the glorious gospel of Christ, who is the image of God, should shine unto them."* – 2 Corinthians 4:3-4

That is why God is against the fashion, beauty, ephemeral things, music, and manners that the world has to offer, because they stemmed from demonic and devilish mindsets. Loving the things of this world is an enmity with God because it is a way of worshipping the god of this world.

CHAPTER SEVEN

"Ye adulterers and adulteresses, know ye not that the friendship of the world is enmity with God? whosoever therefore will be a friend of the world is the enemy of God." – James 4:4

"Love not the world, neither the things that are in the world. If any man love the world, the love of the Father is not in him. For all that is in the world, the lust of the flesh, and the lust of the eyes, and the pride of life, is not of the Father, but is of the world." – 1 John 2:15-16

Idol worship is one major way the devil has perfected for the kingdom of God not to take root in the hearts of men and women. While the kingdom of God should rule and reign in the hearts of men, the devil through idols of the heart has also set up his kingdom of darkness in the hearts of people too. And the kingdom of light and darkness cannot co-habit together in the same heart. One will have to give way for the other.

Idol worship is one of the insidious sins hindering the manifestation of God's kingdom in the heart, lives of many Christians and in several communities today. That is why the scripture repeatedly warn Christians to flee from idolatry.

"Wherefore, my dearly beloved, flee from idolatry." – 1 Corinthians 10:14

> *"Little children, keep yourselves from idols. Amen."* – 1 John 5:21

Today there are national, city, town, village, community, family and personal idols. People look for something to worship and obey than God. In the name of cultural revival, lots of communities and nations are celebrating idols on a national scale in the films and festivals; and holidays are declared to venerate idols. Just as king Nebuchadnezzar set up an idol of gold to be worshipped by the whole world then, the devil has also set up spiritual and personal idols for people to worship at various places.

> *"Thou, O king, hast made a decree, that every man that shall hear the sound of the cornet, flute, harp, sackbut, psaltery, and dulcimer, and all kinds of musick, shall fall down and worship the golden image: And whoso falleth not down and worshippeth, that he should be cast into the midst of a burning fiery furnace."* – Daniel 3:10-11

People bow down, make obeisance, offer sacrifices, rituals, and oblations and hallow their images, effigies and have places devoted to them such as lands, temples, forests and high places.

> *"Whereupon the king took counsel, and made two calves of gold, and said unto them, It is too much for you*

> *to go up to Jerusalem: behold thy gods, O Israel, which brought thee up out of the land of Egypt."* – 1 Kings 12:28

> *"And Israel joined himself unto Baalpeor: and the anger of the LORD was kindled against Israel."* – Numbers 25:3

> *"Now while Paul waited for them at Athens, his spirit was stirred in him, when he saw the city wholly given to idolatry."* – Acts 17:16

Idols of The Heart

It was John Calvin who said that the heart of man is an idol factory. While many people detest physical worship of idols today, yet the truth is that they have idols in their hearts. Personal idols of the heart are the perfect strategy of Satan to rule the life of many and hinder the kingdom of God.

> *"Therefore speak unto them, and say unto them, Thus saith the Lord GOD; Every man of the house of Israel that setteth up his idols in his heart, and putteth the stumblingblock of his iniquity before his face, and cometh to the prophet; I the LORD will answer him that cometh according to the multitude of his idols;"* – Ezekiel 14:4

It is possible to have the fear of God and still serve your idols, one way or the other.

> *"They feared the LORD, and served their own gods, after the manner of the nations whom they carried away from thence. Unto this day they do after the former manners: they fear not the LORD, neither do they after their statutes, or after their ordinances, or after the law and commandment which the LORD commanded the children of Jacob, whom he named Israel;"* – 2 Kings 17:33-34

Too many professing Christians today who seem to have the fear of God by attending churches weekly are nevertheless idol worshippers one way or the other!

What is An Idol?

An idol is an image you worship, venerate and obey. An idol is something that replaces God in your heart and an idol could be God's blessing in your life that has now assumed much more importance than God. Under these three definitions, lots of people are idol worshippers. Today, lots of people, even preachers worship the;

- god of pleasure – lovers of pleasure more than lovers of God.
- god of football – fanatic devotion to the god of soccer.
- god of food – worshipping food more than anything else.
- god of sex – defying human bodies and slaves of bodily appetite.
- god of angels – praying to and venerating the host of heaven.
- god of money – can kill and sell their souls for money.
- god of job – worshipping job and holding it higher than anything else.
- god of career – taking career more vital than God.
- god of children – holding children as the highest.
- god of husband – venerating the husband more than God.
- god of wife – seeing the wife as the only life safer.
- god of properties – going to any extent to acquire and keep properties.
- god of success – seeing success as the ultimate in life.
- god of ministry – seeing the ministry as being more important than the God who gave the ministry.

I have seen people literally bowing down to each of these idols and sacrifice their life, time, heart, emotion, bodies and values for them.

"And the people gave a shout, saying, It is the voice of a god, and not of a man." – Acts 12:22

"And when the people saw what Paul had done, they lifted up their voices, saying in the speech of Lycaonia, The gods are come down to us in the likeness of men." – Acts 14:11

"Howbeit they looked when he should have swollen, or fallen down dead suddenly: but after they had looked a great while, and saw no harm come to him, they changed their minds, and said that he was a god." – Acts 28:6

"But I say, that the things which the Gentiles sacrifice, they sacrifice to devils, and not to God: and I would not that ye should have fellowship with devils." – 1 Corinthians 10:20

"Trust not in oppression, and become not vain in robbery: if riches increase, set not your heart upon them." – Psalm 62:10

*"Their idols are silver and gold, the work of men's hands. They have mouths, but they speak not: eyes have they, but they see not: They have ears, but they hear not: noses

have they, but they smell not: They have hands, but they handle not: feet have they, but they walk not: neither speak they through their throat. They that make them are like unto them; so is every one that trusteth in them." – Psalm 115:4-8

The preachers and Christians of today are surely worshipping these idols with their preaching, emphasis and lifestyles! Small wonder, God's kingdom is not manifesting!

"Their sorrows shall be multiplied that hasten after another god: their drink offerings of blood will I not offer, nor take up their names into my lips." – Psalm 16:4

The scripture is clear as to the consequences of serving idols. Among them are;

- Multiplied sorrows in every area.
- God's fiery wrath, judgment and detestation.
- Bondage and captivity of every sort.
- Being forsaken by all that is good and godly.

"For Israel slideth back as a backsliding heifer: now the LORD will feed them as a lamb in a large place. Ephraim is joined to idols: let him alone." – Hosea 4:16-17;

"Israel hath cast off the thing that is good: the enemy shall pursue him.

> *For Israel hath forgotten his Maker, and buildeth temples; and Judah hath multiplied fenced cities: but I will send a fire upon his cities, and it shall devour the palaces thereof."* –
> Hosea 8:3, 14.

This is the perpetual sin of Israel and God's judgment did not fail to come upon them each time, so also the people of God today. As long as we have cherished idols in our hearts that we secretly worship, God's judgment will keep on falling upon us.

Once an idol displaces God in your heart and robs Him of His glory, it will lead to His judgment upon you. God hates every form of idols and will fight it wherever it is found.

> *"Thou shalt not make unto thee any graven image, or any likeness of any thing that is in heaven above, or that is in the earth beneath, or that is in the water under the earth:"* – Exodus 20:4;

In the kingdom, God must be number one in the heart and life of every citizen. There must be no competition or contending god, fighting for a place in your heart. He can't share your heart with any other graven image. Until He has the whole of you, He won't settle for less. Your body, soul and spirit must belong wholly unto Him. And until God, His word and Spirit are enthroned permanently and above every other thing in your heart and life, you are not free from idols.

Idols come easy but go hard. Idols don't go on their own, unless they are pulled down. And that is the purpose of God's kingdom in the world – to tear down all the vestige of idols in our hearts, society and family. Wherever the kingdom truly comes into, idols must bow and be destroyed permanently, and the will of God must be done whole heartedly on earth, as it is in heaven.

Chapter Eight
KINGDOM WARFARE

Quite sad that many professed believers of today don't realize that we are involved in a spiritual warfare. Many have thought and have been taught from the secular motivational perspectives only, and are very ignorant of the spiritual truth that believers are engaged in a spiritual warfare. The Christian life is not a play ground but a battle ground, more so, the Christian ministry.

A fundamental premise for understanding the warfare of the kingdoms is the biblical teaching of satanic kingdom of darkness.

> *"Wherein in time past ye walked according to the course of this world, according to the prince of the power of the air, the spirit that now worketh in the children of disobedience:"* – Ephesians 2:2

CHAPTER EIGHT

> *"But if our gospel be hid, it is hid to them that are lost: In whom the god of this world hath blinded the minds of them which believe not, lest the light of the glorious gospel of Christ, who is the image of God, should shine unto them."* – 2 Corinthians 4:3-4

> *"And we know that we are of God, and the whole world lieth in wickedness."* – 1 John 5:19

Satan is the ruler of this evil empire, ably assisted by principalities, powers and rulers of darkness of this dark world.

> *"Far above all principality, and power, and might, and dominion, and every name that is named, not only in this world, but also in that which is to come:"* - Ephesians 1:21

> *"For we wrestle not against flesh and blood, but against principalities, against powers, against the rulers of the darkness of this world, against spiritual wickedness in high places."* – Ephesians 6:12

> *"For by him were all things created, that are in heaven, and that are in earth, visible and invisible, whether they be thrones, or dominions, or

> *principalities, or powers: all things were created by him, and for him:"* –
> Colossians 1:16

He opposed God and everything good, just and pure. That is the reason the Bible commands believers not to love the world and the things of the world, because they originated from Satan and they are baits for the believers.

> *"Love not the world, neither the things that are in the world. If any man love the world, the love of the Father is not in him. For all that is in the world, the lust of the flesh, and the lust of the eyes, and the pride of life, is not of the Father, but is of the world. And the world passeth away, and the lust thereof: but he that doeth the will of God abideth for ever."* – 1 John 2:15-17

The authority of Satan over the world is counterfeit and temporary, yet it is real and awesome.

> *"To open their eyes, and to turn them from darkness to light, and from the power of Satan unto God, that they may receive forgiveness of sins, and inheritance among them which are sanctified by faith that is in me."* –
> Acts 26:18

The coming of Christ and His demonstration of kingdom power (1 John 3:8) produced an alarm in the devil's empire (Matthew 4:3; 12:29; Mark 1:24) and a warfare began (Matthew 4:1-11; 16:22-23).

That warfare is still raging till today. The kingdom of darkness, represented by Satan and his demonic agents are still waging war against believers today through temptations to sin and evil, persecutions, hatred, flesh, demonic oppression and pressure to compromise their faith in a corrupt world.

> *"If ye were of the world, the world would love his own: but because ye are not of the world, but I have chosen you out of the world, therefore the world hateth you."* – John 15:19;

> *"I have given them thy word; and the world hath hated them, because they are not of the world, even as I am not of the world."* – John 17:14

> *"But I fear, lest by any means, as the serpent beguiled Eve through his subtilty, so your minds should be corrupted from the simplicity that is in Christ."* - 2 Corinthians 11:3

> *"Whereas angels, which are greater in power and might, bring not railing accusation against them before the Lord."* – 2 Peter 2:11

> *"Be sober, be vigilant; because your adversary the devil, as a roaring*

lion, walketh about, seeking whom he may devour:" – 1 Peter 5:8

Satan hates the church with passion and will do everything to corrupt and incapacitate her. He knew that the church is the only power that can conquer him, so he fights the church both from within and without. He wages warfare against the church through witchcraft manipulations, false doctrines, secular preachers, immorality, worldly-mindedness and love of pleasures, gold and things of this world. Unfortunately, Satan is succeeding too much in his nefarious warfare and many church leaders are deceived and destroyed.

> *"That no man should be moved by these afflictions: for yourselves know that we are appointed thereunto. For verily, when we were with you, we told you before that we should suffer tribulation; even as it came to pass, and ye know. For this cause, when I could no longer forbear, I sent to know your faith, lest by some means the tempter have tempted you, and our labour be in vain."* – 1 Thessalonians 3:3-5

Jesus gave believers the authority to cast out demons, heal the sick, raise the dead and wage victorious warfare against the kingdom of darkness (Mark 4:14-15; Luke 9:1-2; 10:17-19; Acts 5:16).

CHAPTER EIGHT

Believers are not to sit on the fence, but engage in this warfare. Believers are to hate sin, do the will of God and seek to destroy the works of the devil in their lives and society. As a believer and a citizen of His kingdom, there must be no room for the devil in your heart and life. His property must not be in your life, whenever he comes checking.

> *"Hereafter I will not talk much with you: for the prince of this world cometh, and hath nothing in me."* - John 14:30

It then you can wage warfare with your spiritual weapons, which are mighty to pull down strongholds of the enemy everywhere.

> *"(For the weapons of our warfare are not carnal, but mighty through God to the pulling down of strong holds;) Casting down imaginations, and every high thing that exalteth itself against the knowledge of God, and bringing into captivity every thought to the obedience of Christ;"*
> – 2 Corinthians 10:4-5

The kingdom of darkness through traditional religion, occultic covenants, juju covens, herbalists, ancestral worship, demonic rituals, ceremonies, sacrifices, occultic altars, demonic pulpits and fake preachers, prophets and humanistic doctrines are waging serious warfare against the progress and expansion of the kingdom into areas, regions, communities, states, nations and hearts of men and women today.

Genuine believers must therefore rise up and take their God-given responsibilities to defeat and destroy these onslaughts so that the kingdom of God might advance in our time.

CHAPTER EIGHT

Chapter Nine
THE CHURCH AND THE KINGDOM

The more I teach and study the Bible, the more I see the high ignorance of believers and especially church leaders, preachers and ministers about the kingdom. Many believe that the kingdom of God and the church are one and the same. Small wonder that many believes that their church is the kingdom of God and anyone that leaves their church has automatically left the kingdom of God. What a height of ignorance!

The need to have proper understanding of the church and the kingdom is high today, because it has the tendency to correct most of our unhealthy practices.

The church is part of the kingdom, not the whole. Jesus started the church (Matthew 16:18) during His earthly ministry and officially launched her on the day of Pentecost (Acts 2:1-4), but the disciples have become citizens of His kingdom before then (John 13:7-10).

They were saved, washed and given authority to cast out devils (Luke 10:17-20). Therefore, the kingdom preceded the church and larger than the church. The kingdom in heaven will swallow up the church. The church is inside the kingdom, from the beginning to end. You have to become a citizen of the kingdom first, before you can be a bonafide member of the church.

The church is the physical expression of the spiritual kingdom of God, but there are many things that God is doing in the kingdom, outside the four walls of the church. The church and the kingdom overlap. The church is part of the kingdom but the kingdom is much bigger than the church. There are places in the world where the physical expression of the church is not allowed, but the kingdom is there. For example, it is possible to be in the church and yet, not be a citizen of His kingdom.

Today there are many churches that are not kingdom churches. There are preachers who have their pulpits but are not citizens of His kingdom. There are church members who have membership cards, positions and titles, but are not saved, living righteous and Christ-like lives. They are known in the church but unknown in His kingdom. Church members who are wicked, religious, demonized, immoral, corrupt and ungodly are not citizens of His kingdom.

> *"Know ye not that the unrighteous shall not inherit the kingdom of*

God? Be not deceived: neither fornicators, nor idolaters, nor adulterers, nor effeminate, nor abusers of themselves with mankind, Nor thieves, nor covetous, nor drunkards, nor revilers, nor extortioners, shall inherit the kingdom of God." – 1 Corinthians 6:9-10.

Kingdom citizens are those who have encountered Christ, become transformed and who bring forth the fruits of righteousness in their daily lives and living.

"Therefore say I unto you, The kingdom of God shall be taken from you, and given to a nation bringing forth the fruits thereof." – Matthew 21:43

"For the kingdom of God is not meat and drink; but righteousness, and peace, and joy in the Holy Ghost." - Romans 14:17

It is church members that hide under grace to live wayward lives and use the grace of God as license for lascivious lifestyle. But kingdom citizens appropriate the grace of God to live holily, righteously and justly in this present world.

"For the grace of God that bringeth salvation hath appeared to all men, Teaching us that, denying ungodliness and worldly lusts, we

CHAPTER NINE

should live soberly, righteously, and godly, in this present world;" - Titus 2:11-12.

Kingdom citizens are not nominal Christians who only practice religion, but true devotees of Christ who are living as light and salt in the world. They are now tribe and nation of God.

Today, there are many amazing names and expressions of the church, which on one hand is good and praise worthy, but on the other hand are not encouraging, because they are contraptions of men. Lots of such churches today are simply religious centers that worship 'men of God' and not actually kingdom churches.

Many have started and founded churches today on humanistic ideas, secular issues, motivational talks and modern strategies. Such churches are not His church because they don't preach Jesus, kingdom gospel, nor get people saved, transformed and translated from darkness to light. Rather, they joined the devil to damn souls with false teachings that allow, pamper, and encourage sins, immoral living and worldliness.

Kingdom churches are built on Christ, His eternal word and Spirit. Kingdom churches are populated by kingdom citizens who are living kingdom lifestyles. In kingdom churches, Jesus is the true Lord, He is lifted up and His will is paramount in the ways things are being done.

Kingdom churches are not planted due to the motive of money, competition and personal empire, but they are for soul winning and raising kingdom disciples that will go on to expand and extend the kingdom of God in the world through their gifts, graces and ministries.

CHAPTER NINE

Chapter Ten

GOSPEL OF THE KINGDOM

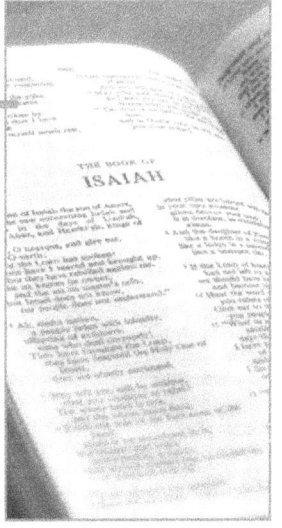

A certain preacher was sent by the Lord to start a church in an unreached place. He went there with zeal and passion to bring people to the Lord. After some few years, he discovered that people were not responding as fast as he envisaged and he was advised by fellow preachers to change his preaching and preach what the people want to hear. He did so and crowd flocked to his church. The money also started rolling in and a large edifice was built and things were going great materially and physically. But down within he was unsatisfied and discovered to his chagrin that majority of the people were not saved, even though very religious, as they daily displayed traits that show that they don't know the Lord.

Upon this discovery, the Pastor started seeking the Lord afresh and he was made to realize where he had missed it. Specifically, the Lord told him that "it is only the kingdom gospel that can truly change and transform people, not any other gospel". He repented and went back to preaching the gospel of the kingdom in the power of the Holy Spirit, and transformations started taking place in the lives of the people again.

Gospel of the Kingdom

Jesus Christ came and proclaimed the gospel of the kingdom. He did not only proclaim it, He demonstrated it.

> *"And Jesus went about all Galilee, teaching in their synagogues, and preaching the gospel of the kingdom, and healing all manner of sickness and all manner of disease among the people."* – Matthew 4:23

> *"And this gospel of the kingdom shall be preached in all the world for a witness unto all nations; and then shall the end come."* – Matthew 24:14

The gospel of the kingdom is to be heard and experienced. In scriptural sense, what is the gospel of the kingdom? The gospel of the kingdom is the good news of the coming, suffering, death and triumphant resurrection of Christ. It is the gospel of repentance from dead works and turning to serve the living God. It is the gospel of obtaining salvation through belief in the atoning work of Christ and living a holy, righteous, sanctified and Christ-like life in this present world. It is the gospel of victorious works.

> *"The Spirit of the Lord is upon me, because he hath anointed me to preach the gospel to the poor; he hath sent me to heal the brokenhearted, to preach deliverance to the captives, and recovering of sight to the blind, to set at liberty them that are bruised, To preach the acceptable year of the Lord."* – Luke 4:18-19.

It is the gospel of power demonstration, demonstrating the power of God over Satan by casting out devils, healing the sick, raising the dead, cleansing the lepers and generally performing miracles, signs and wonders.

> *"And when Jesus was come into Peter's house, he saw his wife's mother laid, and sick of a fever. And he touched her hand, and the fever left her: and she arose, and ministered unto them. When the even was come, they brought unto him many that were possessed with devils: and he cast out the spirits with his word, and healed all that were sick:"* – Matthew 8:14-16

> *"And at even, when the sun did set, they brought unto him all that were diseased, and them that were possessed with devils. And all the city was gathered together at the door. And he healed many that were*

> *sick of divers diseases, and cast out many devils; and suffered not the devils to speak, because they knew him."* – Mark 1:32-34

> *"How God anointed Jesus of Nazareth with the Holy Ghost and with power: who went about doing good, and healing all that were oppressed of the devil; for God was with him."* – Acts 10:38

It is the gospel of heaven, return and eternal kingdom of Christ. That was the gospel that Jesus preached and demonstrated. The Apostles also preached this gospel of the kingdom and preachers today cannot but go back to preaching this gospel. Our Lord Jesus commissioned His Apostles to proclaim and demonstrate the gospel of the kingdom everywhere they go.

> *"Then he called his twelve disciples together, and gave them power and authority over all devils, and to cure diseases. And he sent them to preach the kingdom of God, and to heal the sick. And he said unto them, Take nothing for your journey, neither staves, nor scrip, neither bread, neither money; neither have two coats apiece."* – Luke 9:1-3

> *"And the seventy returned again with joy, saying, Lord, even the devils are subject unto us through*

thy name. And he said unto them, I beheld Satan as lightning fall from heaven. Behold, I give unto you power to tread on serpents and scorpions, and over all the power of the enemy: and nothing shall by any means hurt you." – Luke 10:17-19

"How God anointed Jesus of Nazareth with the Holy Ghost and with power: who went about doing good, and healing all that were oppressed of the devil; for God was with him." – Acts 10:38

The miracles, healings and supernatural demonstrations were to authenticate the word that was being spoken. They are to demonstrate the power and presence of God among His people, and the Book of Acts shows that this is what the first disciples did. Kingdom ministers today must preach the kingdom gospel.

Another Gospel

A cursory look at many pulpits today will reveal that another gospel is what is being preached. Majority of preachers, just like the opening story of this chapter have dabbled into preaching corrupt versions, twisted versions or false versions of the gospel of the kingdom. Today, you hear much of gospel of money, gain, prosperity, fame, feel good and humanistic, secular teachings that dwells much on gaining the ephemeral things of this life than the true gospel of the kingdom.

Today, preachers preach what suits them, so as to gain fame, worship and pocket of the people and totally neglect to preach the true gospel of the kingdom. The more reason we have much more sinners, religious, unsaved, secular and ungodly people filling our pews in large numbers today.

It's time that every minister, Pastor and preacher goes back to preaching and demonstrating the gospel of the kingdom. It is the wholesome, balanced and matured preaching of the kingdom gospel that God will back up and support with His power. God will only confirm His gospel with supernatural power and demonstrations, not our own warped gospels. We must use our pulpits to pull people out of their pits of sin, evil and dooms.

> *"And he said unto them, Go ye into all the world, and preach the gospel to every creature. And they went forth, and preached every where, the Lord working with them, and confirming the word with signs following."* – Mark 16:15, 20.

When you fail to preach the gospel of the kingdom, the power of the Holy Spirit will not back you up and you will have to look for your own power. That is why we have the high incidences of preachers using fake powers, occultic manipulations, prophetic gimmicks and mumbo-jumbo, and witchcraft to perform spurious miracles today. It is sure that the power and gifts of the Holy Spirit will never be there to confirm another gospel other than the gospel of the kingdom.

> *"But as we were allowed of God to be put in trust with the gospel, even so we speak; not as pleasing men, but God, which trieth our hearts. For neither at any time used we flattering words, as ye know, nor a cloke of covetousness; God is witness:"* - 1 Thessalonians 2:4-5

If you are a kingdom-minister, you will preach the kingdom gospel in the power of the Holy Spirit. That is what we are commissioned to preach and demonstrate. It is only the gospel of the kingdom that will liberate, change and transform people and the world. Any other gospel will ruin and destroy now and later.

> *"And my speech and my preaching was not with enticing words of man's wisdom, but in demonstration of the Spirit and of power: That your faith should not stand in the wisdom of men, but in the power of God."* – 1 Corinthians 2:4-5.

CHAPTER TEN

Chapter Eleven

KINGDOM PRAYING

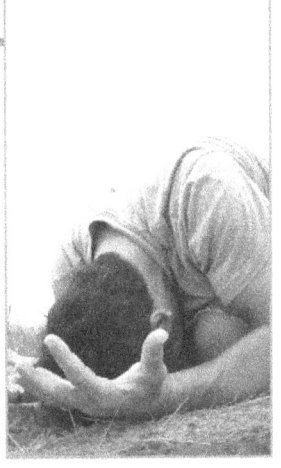

Jesus Christ our Lord and Master specifically taught here that we should pray for the coming and manifestation of the kingdom of God in the world.

> *"After this manner therefore pray ye: Our Father which art in heaven, Hallowed be thy name. Thy kingdom come. Thy will be done in earth, as it is in heaven."* – Matthew 9-10.

Our constant and regular prayer should be "let thy kingdom come". Even though there is a future aspect to the kingdom of God or heaven, as I have explained in previous chapters, yet there is the immediate aspect of the manifestation of God's kingdom that requires our serious and earnest prayers. A strong premise to understand this truth is that Satan is the prince of this world – the systems, values and cosmos spirit directing the affairs of men.

CHAPTER ELEVEN

> *"Hereafter I will not talk much with you: for the prince of this world cometh, and hath nothing in me."* – John 14:30

> *"Now is the judgment of this world: now shall the prince of this world be cast out."* – John 12:31

> *"Wherein in time past ye walked according to the course of this world, according to the prince of the power of the air, the spirit that now worketh in the children of disobedience:"* – Ephesians 2:2

Satan has a counterfeit and temporary kingdom and power in place here in the world and he got that authority due to the sin of Adam in the Garden of Eden. God is bound by moral right and has therefore limited Himself in the affairs of the world since Adam sold our rights to Satan.

> *"And the devil said unto him, All this power will I give thee, and the glory of them: for that is delivered unto me; and to whomsoever I will I give it. If thou therefore wilt worship me, all shall be thine."* – Luke 4:6-7.

Satan acknowledged it and our Lord Jesus did not dispute it with Satan. To intervene and destroy the counterfeit authority of Satan, man would have to take it back, because it was man that gave it to Satan in the first place.

Jesus came as a man (the last Adam), defeated Satan first in the wilderness and finally on the cross, and took the authority back.

> *"And Jesus came and spake unto them, saying, All power is given unto me in heaven and in earth."* – Matthew 28:18

Satan counterfeits His authority and thereby his kingdom can be invaded, and captives set free.

> *"And having spoiled principalities and powers, he made a shew of them openly, triumphing over them in it."* – Colossians 2:15

> *"Which he wrought in Christ, when he raised him from the dead, and set him at his own right hand in the heavenly places, Far above all principality, and power, and might, and dominion, and every name that is named, not only in this world, but also in that which is to come: And hath put all things under his feet, and gave him to be the head over all things to the church,"* – Ephesians 1:20-22.

The demonstration and manifestation of God's kingdom here on earth depends to a great degree on our prayers. Our prayers give God the platform to intervene in the affairs of men. God cannot do anything without our prayers. Kingdom power will only be manifested based on our prayer and petitions.

> *"Verily I say unto you, Whatsoever ye shall bind on earth shall be bound in heaven: and whatsoever ye shall loose on earth shall be loosed in heaven."* – Matthew 18:18

The action starts here and then heaven will respond. The territories that Satan has gained will be retaken and his counterfeit power destroyed only if the saints learn to stand on the finished work of Christ and resist, bind, plunder, destroy and overcome the power of darkness through our prayers.

> *"And the seventy returned again with joy, saying, Lord, even the devils are subject unto us through thy name. And he said unto them, I beheld Satan as lightning fall from heaven. Behold, I give unto you power to tread on serpents and scorpions, and over all the power of the enemy: and nothing shall by any means hurt you"*. - Luke 10:17-19

> *"Submit yourselves therefore to God. Resist the devil, and he will flee from you"*. - James 4:7

> *"The strangers shall fade away, and be afraid out of their close places"*. - Psalm 18:45.

It is in answer to the prayer requests of the believers that God will display His supernatural power in the affairs of men. But if we are prayerless and powerless, God will be incapacitated from working. If we truly want to see God at work, then each believer must take up the responsibility of praying "let thy kingdom come into the territories of our lives, homes, hearts, churches, areas, streets, communities and cities. Then we can see the destruction of the kingdom of darkness as our prayers are intensified and prevailed.

> *"Then Philip went down to the city of Samaria, and preached Christ unto them. And the people with one accord gave heed unto those things which Philip spake, hearing and seeing the miracles which he did. For unclean spirits, crying with loud voice, came out of many that were possessed with them: and many taken with palsies, and that were lame, were healed. And there was great joy in that city."* – Acts 8:5-8

> *"And I will give unto thee the keys of the kingdom of heaven: and whatsoever thou shalt bind on earth shall be bound in heaven: and whatsoever thou shalt loose on earth shall be loosed in heaven."* – Matthew 16:19

The kingdom of Satan, manifested by sin, evils, sicknesses, poverty, diseases, violence and numerous evils and wickedness will be destroyed and overcome when the saints learn to draw down the hand of God through their prayers.

Recently, a minister went to the hospital to pray for his seriously sick sister. She was already dying and saying her goodbyes. This minister stood in prayer for her right there. After some few hours, she woke up and said she saw her spirit flew out of her body and going up but someone stopped her and said, "Your brother is praying and you must go back". That was how she returned and she was healed.

Kingdom Praying

Kingdom praying is prevailing and victorious praying. It is praying with a pure heart and faith in the atoning work of Christ. It is putting on the whole armour of God while praying, pleading the blood of Christ and standing on scriptural grounds.

> *"And these signs shall follow them that believe; In my name shall they cast out devils; they shall speak with new tongues;"* - Mark 16:17
>
> *"Behold, I give unto you power to tread on serpents and scorpions, and over all the power of the enemy: and nothing shall by any means hurt you."* - Luke 10:19

It is resisting the enemy, binding, plundering and destroying the works of the devil through the powerful name of Jesus. It is praying according to the leading of the Holy Spirit and in our spiritual prayer languages.

> *"But if I cast out devils by the Spirit of God, then the kingdom of God is come unto you."* - Matthew 12:28

Praying 'Let thy kingdom come' is not optional for Christians. It is mandatory if we are to see God at work in our lives and cities. We must bring the kingdom of God into every area of our lives and church, it is then we can reign.

> *"To him that overcometh will I grant to sit with me in my throne, even as I also overcame, and am set down with my Father in his throne."* - Revelation 3:21

CHAPTER ELEVEN

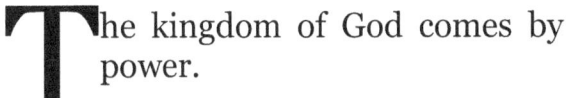

KINGDOM POWER

The kingdom of God comes by power.

"For the kingdom of God is not in word, but in power." - 1 Corinthians 4:20

The kingdom of God will always manifest through power demonstration. The power of the kingdom is the Holy Spirit of God.

"But ye shall receive power, after that the Holy Ghost is come upon you: and ye shall be witnesses unto me both in Jerusalem, and in all Judaea, and in Samaria, and unto the uttermost part of the earth." - Acts 1:8

And our gospel can only become the gospel of power if we are truly filled and endued with the Holy Spirit sent down from heaven.

CHAPTER TWELVE

> *"Unto whom it was revealed, that not unto themselves, but unto us they did minister the things, which are now reported unto you by them that have preached the gospel unto you with the Holy Ghost sent down from heaven; which things the angels desire to look into."* – 1 Peter 1:12

The Holy Spirit anoints and empowers so that we can demonstrate the kingdom of God over that of Satan. The gospel of the kingdom, when preached under the anointing and infilling of the power of the Holy Spirit cannot but result in miracles, signs and wonders.

> *"How God anointed Jesus of Nazareth with the Holy Ghost and with power: who went about doing good, and healing all that were oppressed of the devil; for God was with him."* - Acts 10:38

Jesus categorically stated that signs and wonders will confirm the message.

> *"So Jesus came again into Cana of Galilee, where he made the water wine. And there was a certain nobleman, whose son was sick at Capernaum. When he heard that Jesus was come out of Judaea into Galilee, he went unto him, and besought him that he would come*

down, and heal his son: for he was at the point of death. Then said Jesus unto him, Except ye see signs and wonders, ye will not believe. The nobleman saith unto him, Sir, come down ere my child die. Jesus saith unto him, Go thy way; thy son liveth. And the man believed the word that Jesus had spoken unto him, and he went his way. And as he was now going down, his servants met him, and told him, saying, Thy son liveth. Then enquired he of them the hour when he began to amend. And they said unto him, Yesterday at the seventh hour the fever left him. So the father knew that it was at the same hour, in the which Jesus said unto him, Thy son liveth: and himself believed, and his whole house. This is again the second miracle that Jesus did, when he was come out of Judaea into Galilee." - John 4:46-54.

"Verily, verily, I say unto you, He that believeth on me, the works that I do shall he do also; and greater works than these shall he do; because I go unto my Father." - John 14:12

The signs were to attest to the veracity of the word and to make known that we come from God.

CHAPTER TWELVE

The New Testament church experienced rapid growth due to the fact that signs and wonders attested to their preaching through the power of the Holy Spirit (Acts 5:12-16; 6-8). The church was established and spread to many places as a result of power demonstration.

Apostle Paul attributed his success in ministry to the demonstration of the power of the Spirit in signs and wonders.

> *"Through mighty signs and wonders, by the power of the Spirit of God; so that from Jerusalem, and round about unto Illyricum, I have fully preached the gospel of Christ. Yea, so have I strived to preach the gospel, not where Christ was named, lest I should build upon another man's foundation:"* - Romans 15:19-20

> *"And my speech and my preaching was not with enticing words of man's wisdom, but in demonstration of the Spirit and of power: That your faith should not stand in the wisdom of men, but in the power of God."* - 1 Corinthians 2:4-5

> *" For our gospel came not unto you in word only, but also in power, and in the Holy Ghost, and in much assurance; as ye know what manner of men we were among you for your*

sake." – 1 Thessalonians 1:5

"How shall we escape, if we neglect so great salvation; which at the first began to be spoken by the Lord, and was confirmed unto us by them that heard him; God also bearing them witness, both with signs and wonders, and with divers miracles, and gifts of the Holy Ghost, according to his own will?" – Hebrews 2:3-4

It is the presence and power of the Spirit in our lives that will give power to our words and prayers. The absence of the Holy Spirit in our lives translates to powerless living and powerless works.

The great key to the demonstration of the kingdom gospel is the outpouring of the Holy Spirit.

"And when the day of Pentecost was fully come, they were all with one accord in one place. And suddenly there came a sound from heaven as of a rushing mighty wind, and it filled all the house where they were sitting. And there appeared unto them cloven tongues like as of fire, and it sat upon each of them. And they were all filled with the Holy Ghost, and began to speak with other tongues, as the Spirit gave them utterance." - Acts 2:1-4

CHAPTER TWELVE

"The grace of the Lord Jesus Christ, and the love of God, and the communion of the Holy Ghost, be with you all. Amen." - 2 Corinthians 13:14

"In the last day, that great day of the feast, Jesus stood and cried, saying, If any man thirst, let him come unto me, and drink. He that believeth on me, as the scripture hath said, out of his belly shall flow rivers of living water. (But this spake he of the Spirit, which they that believe on him should receive: for the Holy Ghost was not yet given; because that Jesus was not yet glorified.)" - John 7:37-39

Without the outpouring, baptism and infilling of the Holy Spirit in a definite experience, we cannot demonstrate the power of the kingdom.

The baptism of the Holy Spirit, with the initial evidence of speaking in tongues is an experience that every genuine believer must have after salvation and inner cleansing. You must seek the Lord for this experience until you are endued with power from on high, just like the Apostles. Without this experience, you will continue to live defeated lives and unstable in your walk with the Lord.

The Baptism of the Holy Spirit enables you to live a victorious Christian life, empowers you to pray, live in dominion over circumstances, situations and helps you to reign in life. As you get filled with the presence and power of the Holy Spirit, you must maintain a regular and close communion with the Lord in His word and prayers. You must be open to the gifts and graces that the Holy Spirit can bestow. You must submit to the leading and direction of the Spirit of God, as He wants to demonstrate His power through you.

To demonstrate kingdom power, you must recognize that believers don't wrestle against flesh and blood; you must live a life committed to God, truth and righteousness.

> *"For we wrestle not against flesh and blood, but against principalities, against powers, against the rulers of the darkness of this world, against spiritual wickedness in high places"*. - Ephesians 6:12

> *"I beseech you therefore, brethren, by the mercies of God, that ye present your bodies a living sacrifice, holy, acceptable unto God, which is your reasonable service. Therefore if thine enemy hunger, feed him; if he thirst, give him drink: for in so doing thou shalt heap coals of fire on his head"*. - Romans 12:1, 20

CHAPTER TWELVE

You must have the faith that believers are sitting with Christ in heavenly places, far above every principality and powers (Eph. 2:5-6) and we have the authority to dismantle and destroy the power of Satan anywhere and everywhere.

> *"To open their eyes, and to turn them from darkness to light, and from the power of Satan unto God, that they may receive forgiveness of sins, and inheritance among them which are sanctified by faith that is in me".* - Acts 26:18.

You must operate with the reality that our weapon in Christ is mighty to pull down strongholds of the enemy (2 Corinthians 10:4-5). You must continually proclaim the gospel of the kingdom in the power of the Holy Spirit. Always be ready to challenge the power of Satan in Jesus' name (Acts 16:16-18); by the word of God (Ephesians 6:17) by fasting and praying in the Spirit (Matthew 9:29) and by casting out demons in faith (Mark 16:17).

You must constantly pray for and eagerly desire the manifestation of kingdom power through you, to the glory of His name, and not for your personal pride.

Chapter Thirteen
KINGDOM AUTHORITY AND POWER

To proclaim His victory over the kingdom of darkness and to expand the frontiers of His kingdom to every heart and territories, our Lord Jesus gave spiritual authority and power to His disciples.

> *"Then he called his twelve disciples together, and gave them power and authority over all devils, and to cure diseases. And he sent them to preach the kingdom of God, and to heal the sick."* - Luke 9:1-2

He demonstrated the power of His kingdom by casting out devils, heaingl the sick and raising the dead. He promised the same power and authority. He even said His disciples will do the works that He did and greater works.

CHAPTER THIRTEEN

> *"Verily, verily, I say unto you, He that believeth on me, the works that I do shall he do also; and greater works than these shall he do; because I go unto my Father".* - John 14:12.

After His resurrection (Matthew 28:9, 18), having received authority and power from the Father and being raised far above principalities and powers, sat at the right hand of God and poured out His Holy Spirit upon believers.

> *"And hath raised us up together, and made us sit together in heavenly places in Christ Jesus:"* – Ephesians 2:6

> *"Which he wrought in Christ, when he raised him from the dead, and set him at his own right hand in the heavenly places, Far above all principality, and power, and might, and dominion, and every name that is named, not only in this world, but also in that which is to come: And hath put all things under his feet, and gave him to be the head over all things to the church,"* - Ephesians 1:20-22

While power is transferable and transient, authority is invested in people. The 16-tyre truck has the power to speed, push and carry loads, but the Traffic Officer has the invested authority to stop its movement! The authority of the Police Officer is in his uniform, badge and staff. He only needs to raise his hand or issue out an order and the truck with all its power must stop. Furthermore, the king doesn't have to be everywhere, he only needs to send forth his signet or staff of authority and subjects must obey.

In the kingdom of God, every believer has been given authority over sin, Satan and vicissitudes of life through the indwelling Christ (1 John 4:4); Faith in the finished work of Christ on Calvary (1 John 5:4); the word of God (Luke 9:1-2) and by virtue of our position with Christ (Eph. 2:6; 1:20-22).

The positional truth about believers is that we are seated together with Christ in heavenly places, far above principalities and powers. Believers are therefore not to live defeated lives or be prevailed upon by the forces of darkness.

In the kingdom, believers are kings with Christ on the throne and are to live overcoming, victorious and prevailing lives in this present world. Believers are to resist, overcome and prevail over the devil, his demons and evil systems of the world (James 4:7; 1 Peter 5:9; Revelation 3:21).

The degree of our overcoming life must commensurate with that of our Lord Jesus. Believers are to Nikao (Greek word for overcome) the devil and his cohorts in every territory of our lives, families, churches, communities and cities.

If you have been filled with the Spirit of life and power, then you have all the authority to live overcoming life in this world. To demonstrate your God given authority therefore, you must do the following:

1. **Sit with Christ** – Ephesians 2:6

You may not feel it, but that is the scriptural truth about each believer. We have been made to sit with Christ in heavenly places, far above all powers of the enemy. Believers are not under the dominion of Satan, but far above him and can therefore resist him and bind his demons. Believe it and live in that truth everyday.

2. **Walk in the Spirit** – Gal. 5:16-19

Believers must be filled with the Holy Spirit and daily walk according to the leading of the Spirit. To walk in the Spirit is to live in the word of God, regular prayers and to mind things of eternal value. It is to be open to the promptings and leading of the Holy Spirit in every situation. It is to live in obedience to the word of God and overcome all the temptations of the flesh and the world.

3. **Stand in the Truth** – 2 Corinthians 13:8

The authority of God in believer's life will show forth as long as they stand in the truth, stand by the truth, stand for the truth and live in the truth everyday of their lives. Jesus is the Truth and His word is the absolute truth of life.

4. **Overcome** – Rev. 3:21

Believers must overcome and prevail. Your authority must be used to overcome every machinations of the enemy in the lives, places and territories of this life. Victorious and prevailing life is the divine portion of every believer. He causes His people to triumph always.

> *"Now thanks be unto God, which always causeth us to triumph in Christ, and maketh manifest the savour of his knowledge by us in every place."* - 2 Corinthians 2:14

> *"And the God of peace shall bruise Satan under your feet shortly. The grace of our Lord Jesus Christ be with you. Amen."* - Romans 16:20

CHAPTER THIRTEEN

Chapter Fourteen

KINGDOM PURPOSE AND PRINCIPLE

Jesus stated categorically that the purpose of the kingdom in the world is;

> *"Thy will be done on earth, as it is in heaven"* – Matthew 6:10.

The Lord wants His will to be done and obeyed by His creatures, that is why He sent His son into the world (Isaiah 46:9-10). The purpose of the kingdom in the world therefore is basically to reconcile the prodigal world back to the Father. The principle of the kingdom is obedience to the Father and doing His will and obeying His counsel in every area of our lives. Peace with the Father, righteous, obedient lifestyle and joy in His Spirit is the objectives that the kingdom must achieve in every heart, life and nations of the world.

> *"For the kingdom of God is not meat and drink; but righteousness, and*

CHAPTER FOURTEEN

peace, and joy in the Holy Ghost." - Romans 14:17

The world, as we know it, is living in rebellion, disobedience, sin and enmity with God. The world, through the deception of Satan and sin is estranged from the Lord (Rev. 12:9; Romans 7:11). God is angry with the sin of the world and will direct them to hell, unless they repent and turn back to Him (Psalm 7:11; 9:17). Because He doesn't want anyone to go to Hell, God sent His only begotten Son to the world, to die and resurrect and be the atonement for the sin of the world (John 3:17-18).

Whosoever accepts and believe the atoning work of His Son, genuinely repenting and turning away from sin, will be automatically translated from the kingdom of sin and Satan into the kingdom of light, peace, joy and power of God by the mysterious operation of God.

> *"Who hath delivered us from the power of darkness, and hath translated us into the kingdom of his dear Son:"* – Colossians 1:13

Becoming the citizen of His kingdom entitles the believer to all the power, authority and dominion living that can only be found in Christ.

As kingdom citizens therefore, we must live our lives to fulfill the purpose of the kingdom in the world. While we must daily live by the principle of the kingdom, which is complete, prompt, total, unquestionable and continuous obedience to the Lord and His word, we must also pursue the purpose of the kingdom in the world. We must pray and work to bring the purpose of the kingdom to these ten areas of human influence in the world:

1. Family:

The kingdom of God must be in every family. The will of God must be done in every home. The family is a mission field today and we must bring the kingdom of God back into our homes and families. The will of the Lord must be done in the hearts of fathers, mothers and children.

2. Religion:

Religiosity without knowing the true God through His Son Jesus Christ is very rife in the world today. People are religious but devoid of the knowledge of the true God. Even in the church, there is much churchianity without Christ. Too many secular, nominal and unChrist-like people are in Church but not true citizens of His kingdom today. We need to bring the kingdom purpose into every church and religion today.

3. Government:

People in government must be made to fulfill the kingdom purpose. They must rule in a just manner, with the fear of God and justice. Governments must resemble the true government of God. It must be peopled by kingdom citizens who will bring the kingdom principle to light and open display.

4. Education:

The knowledge of God and living in His fear must dominate our educational sector. Today, the educational sector has denied God, took away the knowledge of God from young ones and children, the more reason violence and wickedness have multiplied in the world. Education must be evangelized with the kingdom purpose afresh.

5. Business:

Doing business with ethical standards and kingdom principles is a misnomer today. Businesses promote corruption and evil purposes of Satan. Citizens of the kingdom must bring the kingdom of God and His purpose into the business environment and Board rooms.

6. Economy:

The way money is being pursued, made and spent today surely needs the manifestation of kingdom purpose. Money has surely become the god that majority of the people of the world is worshipping. The kingdom purpose and principle must come to this much needed area of human existence.

7. **Politics:**

People who are involved in politics do it without any iota of the fear of God in their hearts. They display penchant for rituals, cultism and occultism. They rule people by domination and strategic oppression. The kingdom of God must be brought to rule and reign here.

8. **Sports:**

Sports must be cleansed with the principles of the kingdom of God. Fair play, justice and fairness must be enthroned. Sport heroes must no longer be idolized and worshipped. The principles of His kingdom must rule in the heart of sports stakeholders.

9. **Entertainment:**

This industry has spread too much error, horrific examples in songs and lifestyles that have ruined the life and souls of millions in the church. It must be invaded with kingdom purpose and principles.

10. **Media:**

The media must be made to bow down to the principles and purpose of the kingdom of God. Truth must prevail over lies and destructive tendencies.

As citizens of His kingdom, we must fulfill kingdom purpose by making His will to be done in these areas.

CHAPTER FOURTEEN

We must be strategic in our evangelism to these strongholds.

Chapter Fifteen

KINGDOM LIFESTYLE

The eternal purpose of God since the foundation of the world is to have His own people, family and peculiar unto Him. He called out those who will serve Him willingly and genuinely and wants them to be different from the world.

> *"Now therefore, if ye will obey my voice indeed, and keep my covenant, then ye shall be a peculiar treasure unto me above all people: for all the earth is mine:"* - Exodus 19:5-6.

People of the kingdom are those who have their sins forgiven and have been translated from the kingdom of darkness into the kingdom of Christ.

> *"Who hath delivered us from the power of darkness, and hath translated us into the kingdom of his dear Son:"* – Colossians 1:13

They are to live a life of peace with God, righteousness and joy in the Holy Spirit.

> *"For the kingdom of God is not meat and drink; but righteousness, and peace, and joy in the Holy Ghost."* – Romans 14:17.

The lifestyle of the kingdom is that of being different, separate from sinful and fleshly desires of this world. The people of the kingdom are a new tribe, nation and peculiar unto God.

> *"But ye are a chosen generation, a royal priesthood, an holy nation, a peculiar people; that ye should shew forth the praises of him who hath called you out of darkness into his marvellous light:"* – 1 Peter 2:9

Kingdom living is a life of heaven on earth – free from pollutions, corruptions and ungodliness of this world. It is doing the will of God on earth as is being done in heaven.

> *"After this manner therefore pray ye: Our Father which art in heaven, Hallowed be thy name. Thy kingdom come. Thy will be done in earth, as it is in heaven."* – Matthew 6:9-10

Kingdom living is being eternally minded and with godly values in everyday lifestyle. Jesus the King of the kingdom says that citizens of the kingdom are not of this world, as He is not of the world.

> *"I have given them thy word; and the world hath hated them, because they are not of the world, even as I am not of the world."* – John 17:14

This means that their lifestyle must model His and be radically different from that of the world that surrounds them.

Church In The World, World In The Church

Unfortunately, this old time and biblical truth has been neglected, twisted and glossed over by majority of the church and preachers of today. It's pretty hard and difficult to differentiate between the church and the world today. Those who professed to be Christians are not different from their neighbours in their choices and lifestyles. The church is in the world and the love of the world is in the church. The scriptural truth of 1 John chapter 2 verses 15 to 17 has been derided and explained away by preachers in the name of success, prosperity and grace teachings.

Today, Christians compete with the world in fashion, automobiles, mansions, gold, jewelries and immoral lifestyles. Christians divorce, remarry, follow latest fashion, pursue money and live extravagantly like the rest of the world.

The attitudes, characters and choices of so-called Christians are radically different from that of the disciples of the Lord and teachings of the Bible. Small wonder that unbelievers deride the church and refused to get converted because they could see no difference between themselves and those who say they believed in Jesus. The words and sad comment of Indira Ghandi is playing itself out again right before our eyes. He said; "When I read the Bible, I love the Jesus I saw and want to follow Him. But when I looked at the life of those who say they are Christians, I don't want to have anything to do with their Christ"

Kingdom Lifestyle

If we are true citizens of His kingdom, now and for eternity, then we must daily live the kingdom lifestyle. What are the features of kingdom lifestyle?

a.   **Christ-like Living** – 1 John 3:1-3

The deep desire of God is that every believer be fashioned like Christ. Each of us must become like Christ – living holy, pure and become like Him in our attitudes, manners and choices. Living as Christ would live in our time here in this world is the goal of God for every Christian. Christ-like living therefore is kingdom lifestyle.

b.   **Obedient Living** – Eccl. 12:13-14

The lifestyle of the kingdom is to live in implicit and complete obedience to the will of the Father. It is a life of purity (1 Thess. 4:3-8); Faith (John 14:21); Walking in the Spirit (Gal. 5:16); Walking in the light (Romans 13:13; Ephesians 5:8); Love (Matt. 5:43-48); Shinning as light and salt in the world (Matt. 5:13-16); and Separation from the world (Heb. 11:13; 1 Peter 2:11).

c.   **Powerful Living** – Acts 1:8; 2:17-18

Kingdom lifestyle is a life empowered by the Holy Spirit and strengthened to be a blessing to others. It is an overcoming, prevailing, victorious and triumphant life over the situations and circumstances of the world.

d.   **Dominion Living:**

It is a life of dominion over sin, Satan, sicknesses and problems of this world. It is reigning as kings and priests of God over the challenges of this present world.

e.   **Offensive Living** – Ephesians 6:10; Matthew 11:12; II Cor. 16:13

The kingdom lifestyle is not only to be strong in the Lord, which is defensive, but also in the power of His might, which is offensive. We must use our spiritual armour to push back the kingdom of darkness and advance the frontiers of the kingdom of light.

Those who seldom pray, compromise with the world, neglect the word of God and have little spiritual hunger cannot live the lifestyle of the kingdom. Those who are secular, carnal and fleshly in their desires and choices cannot live the kingdom lifestyle and they will be thrown out of the kingdom.

It is only those who are ready to pay the price and ready to conform to the will of God that will be enabled to live the kingdom lifestyle and they are the only ones that will enjoy the benefits of His kingdom, now and in eternity.

Chapter Sixteen
KINGDOM GROWTH

Jesus wants His kingdom to grow and expand. Growth is synonymous with the kingdom. The kingdom might start small in a heart, place and among people, but it must grow, increase and expand.

> *"Another parable put he forth unto them, saying, The kingdom of heaven is like to a grain of mustard seed, which a man took, and sowed in his field: Which indeed is the least of all seeds: but when it is grown, it is the greatest among herbs, and becometh a tree, so that the birds of the air come and lodge in the branches thereof."* - Matthew 13:31-32

The kingdom can start small, however, with time; it must grow and affect the whole place positively.

> *"Another parable spake he unto them; The kingdom of heaven is like*

CHAPTER SIXTEEN

unto leaven, which a woman took, and hid in three measures of meal, till the whole was leavened." - Matthew 13:33

Growth is part and parcel of the kingdom of God in every heart and in the world. The kingdom of God is to depopulate hell to populate heaven. True kingdom growth is not only numerical but also spiritual, physical, quality and quantity growth.

Now, church growth teachings have recognized four types of growth;

a. **Biological Growth:** This type of growth occurs when Christians give birth to children in the church. They are born in the church and grow up to become members of the church. This is biological growth.

b. **Transfer Growth:** This type of growth occurs when Christians transferred their membership from one church to the other. This does not necessarily bring growth to the kingdom, except on special cases.

c. **Nominal Growth:** This type of growth occurs when church leaders use all kinds of gimmick to gather 'customers' and crowds of people to their meeting without getting them converted to the Lord. They are nominal and secular people that do not have vital relationship with the Lord. This doesn't grow the kingdom.

d. **Conversion Growth:** This growth occurs when people are genuinely converted, saved, transformed and changed for the Lord. They are translated from the kingdom of darkness to the kingdom of His dear Son. This is real kingdom growth. Kingdom growth is when the rule and reign of Christ extends to many hearts, lives, homes and communities. Any church could be full, brimming with people and yet no actual kingdom growth is taking place.

Kingdom growth is concerned with the conversion of sinners to Christ. Kingdom growth is when people are growing into true disciples of the Lord. Kingdom growth is what gladdens and glorifies the Father. The growth of the first church was both church growth and kingdom growth. Kingdom growth should be the desire and prayer of every church leader.

To really see kingdom growth in our churches and in the world today would demand the following:

1. **Build The Church On His Vision, Word And Ways**

You must catch God's vision for your local church, use His word as your foundation and follow the ways He directs. That is the way to experience kingdom growth. God is committed to the vision He has given to you and as long as you pursue His vision, not your own personal ambition, He will be with you.

2. Proclaim And Demonstrate The Gospel of The Kingdom

To experience kingdom growth, you must preach, pray and demonstrate the gospel of the kingdom practically in your life and work. As you preach the kingdom gospel, the King over the kingdom will back up the word with His Spirit and power. As the gospel is being demonstrated, the kingdom will expand and extend to hearts here and there.

3. Move In The Power of The Holy Spirit

The Holy Spirit of God is the Spirit of the kingdom. He is the One that was sent down from heaven to expand God's kingdom into hearts and territories.

> *"Unto whom it was revealed, that not unto themselves, but unto us they did minister the things, which are now reported unto you by them that have preached the gospel unto you with the Holy Ghost sent down from heaven; which things the angels desire to look into."* - 1 Peter 1:12

Without Him, there can be no kingdom expansion. You must therefore surrender to the Holy Spirit and allow Him to work through you to grow His kingdom. Without the presence, power, gifts and operations of the Holy Spirit, the kingdom cannot come into the heart or the community.

4. Bind The Powers That Blindfold And Darken Hearts

Kingdom growth demands that believers use their spiritual authority to bind the forces of evil that blindfold people and darken hearts to the gospel of light.

> *"But if our gospel be hid, it is hid to them that are lost: In whom the god of this world hath blinded the minds of them which believe not, lest the light of the glorious gospel of Christ, who is the image of God, should shine unto them."* – 2 Corinthians 4:3-4

We must pray down the kingdom of light into the hearts of people and territories. We must engage in spiritual warfare to release those who are bound and held captive by the enemy of all that is good and well. We must intercede for the lost souls and claim them for Christ.

5. Be Involved In Aggressive Evangelism

Evangelism and soul winning must never be relegated in the church if we are to grow His kingdom. Kingdom expansion can only come through evangelism and soul winning. We must reach out and bring people to the saving knowledge of God. We must make sure the kingdom of God comes within those we evangelize. Outreach to various segments of the society must be strategically planned and pursued.

6. Disciple, Mature And Grow People For Him

Kingdom growth also happens when converts are discipled and grounded in Christ. When believers show much more of the fruits of the Spirit in their daily lives and thereby become godly examples to the watching public, the kingdom will take root in the world. Christians that demonstrate love, kindness, goodness, honesty, self-sacrifice and exemplary conduct everywhere they found themselves are showing to the world the values of the kingdom. And that can only come when they are taught, discipled and grow in the Lord.

> *"A new commandment I give unto you, That ye love one another; as I have loved you, that ye also love one another. By this shall all men know that ye are my disciples, if ye have love one to another."* - John 13:34-35

7. Be Heavenly Minded And Eternity Conscious

Being heavenly and not worldly minded is very vital to kingdom growth.

> ***"If ye then be risen with Christ, seek those things which are above, where Christ sitteth on the right hand of God. Set your affection on things above, not on things on the earth." –***
> Colossians 3:1-2

Setting our affections on heavenly things and being eternity conscious would help us to grow His kingdom in the hearts and lives of people.

By these steps, the kingdom of God will be expanded into hearts that have hitherto been occupied by Satan; and the kingdom of righteousness will grow while that of Satan, sin and evil will diminish.

CHAPTER SIXTEEN

Chapter Seventeen

KINGDOM MANDATE

Jesus stated categorically in Matthew chapter 24 verses 14 that; ***"this gospel of the kingdom shall be preached in all the world for a witness unto all nations, and then shall the end come"***. It is not any other gospel, but the gospel of the kingdom. That is what we must preach round the world.

The gospel of the kingdom is the good news about the coming, death, resurrection and victorious power of Christ over sin, Satan, sicknesses and diseases. It is the gospel of victory and liberty over the bondage and darkness of Satan. That is our mandate and what we must emphasize everywhere we go and wherever we can preach to people. We are not to preach a watered-down version of it but the whole gospel of the kingdom. Whether people like it or not, believe it or not, it is the gospel of the kingdom that we must preach everywhere. That is our kingdom mandate. How do we go about fulfilling this mandate?

CHAPTER SEVENTEEN

1. **Become A Kingdom Citizen**

You can't fully preach the kingdom, if the kingdom is not inside you or you are inside the kingdom. Amazingly, you can be religious, neck deep in church activities and yet not be in the kingdom. The only entrance to the kingdom is through genuine repentance and renunciation of sins and crowning Jesus as the King of your heart and life.

When Jesus takes up full residence in your heart and you are grounded in Him with fruits of righteousness in your daily lives, then you are a citizen of the kingdom. Remaining as citizen is not automatic; you must remain in Jesus and be growing in your faith and spiritual life, it is then you can remain as a citizen of the kingdom.

2. **Live For The Kingdom**

It is imperative that you demonstrate kingdom lifestyle in your daily living. You must imbibe the lifestyle of the kingdom, which is victorious living over sin, Satan and sicknesses; holy and righteous living, peace with everybody and joy in the Holy Spirit. Your life must be different from that of sinners and you must daily show forth the praises of Him who has called you out of darkness into the kingdom of His dear Son.

> *"But ye are a chosen generation, a royal priesthood, an holy nation, a*

peculiar people; that ye should shew forth the praises of him who hath called you out of darkness into his marvellous light". - 1 Peter 2:9

3. Pray His Kingdom Down

Fulfilling our kingdom mandate demands that we must pray constantly for the manifestation of His kingdom in the world.

> *"Thy kingdom come. Thy will be done in earth, as it is in heaven."* – Matthew 6:10

We must pray down His kingdom into the territories of our lives, churches, communities, families and nations. It must be our urgent and importunate prayers. The degree of the manifestation of His kingdom in the world is determined by the degree of our prayers for it. It must therefore be our heart and hard cry every time.

4. Seek His Kingdom

You must seek His kingdom in all you do. Seek to promote His kingdom and live for Him.

> *"But seek ye first the kingdom of God, and his righteousness; and all these things shall be added unto you."* – Matthew 6:33

To seek His kingdom is to be heavenly minded in all your doings. It is to be spiritually minded and hold things of this life loosely. It is to be free from worldliness and worldly pleasures. It is to be focused on eternal issues and not mind earthly things. It is to lay your treasures in heaven and don't allow your hearts to be filled with the gold, dust and pleasure of this world. You seek His kingdom when you consider the reproaches of Christ to be of greater riches than the treasures of Egypt because you seek for a city whose builder and maker is God.

5. Preach His Kingdom

The kingdoms of this world will surely pass and wear away; the empires of men will crumble and be forgotten; only His kingdom will last.

> *"Yea, all kings shall fall down before him: all nations shall serve him. His name shall endure for ever: his name shall be continued as long as the sun: and men shall be blessed in him: all nations shall call him blessed."* – Psalm 72:11, 17

It is mandatory that you preach the gospel of the kingdom to all and sundry within your circle of influence. You extend and expand the kingdom through your preaching and teachings. This everlasting kingdom of Christ demands for your proclamation and publications.

6. Build His Kingdom

You build His kingdom by getting people converted and discipling them for Him. You build His kingdom by raising genuine disciples and ministers of the gospel through your ministry. You build His kingdom by helping people to grow in Him, discover and use their gifts for Him. You build His kingdom by allowing others to discover their God-given ministries and encouraging those ministries to thrive. You build His kingdom by giving chance and platform to others to shine and be heard. You build His kingdom when you are a developer of gifts and not a limiter of potentials of those under and around you.

7. Get Ready For His Kingdom

You can fulfill your kingdom mandate when you watch and pray to get ready for His future kingdom. As you live for Him now, you also watch to be counted worthy to be part of His future kingdom. You do that by not drawing back, nor drifting into your old sins, but continuing steadfastly in Him. By enduring to the end of your faith is the key to get ready for His kingdom.

> *"But he that shall endure unto the end, the same shall be saved."* –
> Matthew 24:13

CHAPTER SEVENTEEN

Chapter Eighteen

KINGDOM MINISTRIES

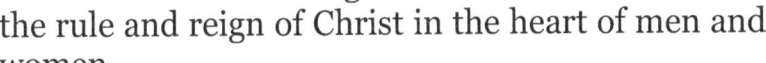

It needs to be stated again that the kingdom of God does not consist only of the future reign of Christ, it is also for now. The present manifestation of the kingdom of God is the rule and reign of Christ in the heart of men and women.

> *"Neither shall they say, Lo here! or, lo there! for, behold, the kingdom of God is within you."* – Luke 17:21

The kingdom is not a religio-political theocracy; it is not a matter of social or political dominions over the nations or kingdoms of this world, rather, it is God coming into the world to assert His power, glory and rights against the dominion of Satan and the present course of this world.

The kingdom is much more than salvation of souls or the church. The kingdom is bigger than the church, even though the church is part of the kingdom. There are many things that God is doing in the world, outside the four walls of the church.

Gifts And Ministries of The Kingdom

God gives gifts to citizens of His kingdom to use, first for His glory and secondly for the expansion of His kingdom.

> *"He said therefore, A certain nobleman went into a far country to receive for himself a kingdom, and to return. And he called his ten servants, and delivered them ten pounds, and said unto them, Occupy till I come. But his citizens hated him, and sent a message after him, saying, We will not have this man to reign over us. And it came to pass, that when he was returned, having received the kingdom, then he commanded these servants to be called unto him, to whom he had given the money, that he might know how much every man had gained by trading. Then came the first, saying, Lord, thy pound hath gained ten pounds. And he said unto him, Well, thou good servant: because thou hast been faithful in a very little, have thou authority over ten cities. And the second came, saying, Lord, thy pound hath gained*

five pounds. And he said likewise to him, Be thou also over five cities. And another came, saying, Lord, behold, here is thy pound, which I have kept laid up in a napkin: For I feared thee, because thou art an austere man: thou takest up that thou layedst not down, and reapest that thou didst not sow. And he saith unto him, Out of thine own mouth will I judge thee, thou wicked servant. Thou knewest that I was an austere man, taking up that I laid not down, and reaping that I did not sow: Wherefore then gavest not thou my money into the bank, that at my coming I might have required mine own with usury? And he said unto them that stood by, Take from him the pound, and give it to him that hath ten pounds. (And they said unto him, Lord, he hath ten pounds.) For I say unto you, That unto every one which hath shall be given; and from him that hath not, even that he hath shall be taken away from him. But those mine enemies, which would not that I should reign over them, bring hither, and slay them before me." – Luke 19:12-27

The servants or citizens of the kingdom were to use their God-given gifts to profit and expand the kingdom of God in this world. Firstly, the gifts or talents were freely given. They did not beg for it but

CHAPTER EIGHTEEN

were given by the sovereignty of the Great Giver.

Secondly, the Giver gave them according to the ability of the recipients, not by favouritism. Thirdly, they are to profit, make use and multiply the gifts by their proper usage. Fourthly, rewards will be based on the proper use and multiplication of the gifts received. And finally, there will be severe punishment for gift-neglect or improper use.

These are principles of the kingdom. Whoever is a citizen of the kingdom must discover and utilize the gifts that he has been given and use them properly for His glory and the expansion of His kingdom here on earth. Every member of the kingdom has at least one gift and you must occupy with that gift for Him. Your reward will be based on the usage of the gifts you have received from Him. You might even be thrown out of the kingdom if you fail to use your gift for Him.

Furthermore, it is the gifts that will eventually become the ministries of the kingdom. Kingdom ministries are the special calling of the Lord in an individual's life to an area, either he or she is a professional minister or not. It is not every ministry that will start or end up in a church. Ministries must exist specially from church.

Kingdom ministry has much to do with the ministry of the saints to various segments of the society. There are many places and people that the church cannot reach, but kingdom ministry will reach those places

and people. Every kingdom citizen is;
* Saved for ministry - we are saved to serve.
* Gifted for ministry - your gift is your ministry.
* Called for ministry - a high and holy calling to an area.
* Commissioned for ministry - commissioned by the Lord Jesus.
* Commanded for ministry - commanded by apostolic authority.
* Authorized for ministry - authorized by our Lord Jesus.
* Anointed for ministry - your anointing is to enable you for ministry
* Rewarded for ministry - your reward will be based on your faithfulness to your ministry.

We have not all been called or gifted to plant, start or lead a local church, but we have all been called and gifted for kingdom ministry. Every kingdom citizen must therefore locate and abide in the ministry God has given Him in the kingdom.

In the expansive vineyard of the Lord, there are many departments and tasks that must be done. It is the same kingdom and vineyard, but different assignments are given to each of us. Some have ministry of and to Youths, Marriage, Family, Children, Drug addicts, Drama, Teaching, Counseling, Writing, Praying, Giving, Prisoners, Deliverance, Singing and Prophetic. You must discern properly your ministry and abide within it for His glory.

CHAPTER EIGHTEEN

"Let every man abide in the same calling wherein he was called." – 1 Corinthians 7:20

Until you strive to fulfill your ministry, you cannot be fulfilled in life. Your success, promotion and upliftment are in your ministry. You can never enjoy God's blessing outside the ministry He has graciously given to you. Locating your ministry is the key to your location. If you don't locate your ministry, you will not be located. Are you in your ministry location or somewhere else?

Chapter Nineteen
KINGDOM HARVEST

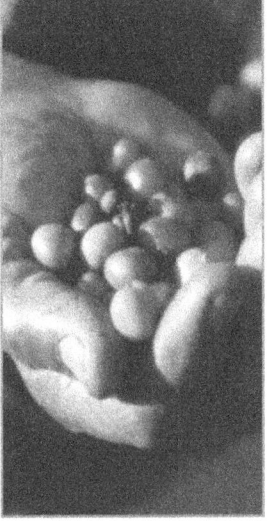

Kingdom harvest is not about bazaar and fruits of the field as some church practices would want us to believe today. It is not about farm produce which are sold at exorbitant prices at the church celebrations once a year, to raise funds. Rather, kingdom harvest is about soul winning and spiritual fruitfulness and impact.

> *"Say not ye, There are yet four months, and then cometh harvest? behold, I say unto you, Lift up your eyes, and look on the fields; for they are white already to harvest."* – John 4:35

The colour of the kingdom is green - growing, fruitful and multiplying. The principle of the kingdom is that of an evergreen tree, bearing fruits all year round and eternally.

CHAPTER NINETEEN

"The righteous shall flourish like the palm tree: he shall grow like a cedar in Lebanon. Those that be planted in the house of the LORD shall flourish in the courts of our God. They shall still bring forth fruit in old age; they shall be fat and flourishing;" – Psalm 92:12-14

"And he shall be like a tree planted by the rivers of water, that bringeth forth his fruit in his season; his leaf also shall not wither; and whatsoever he doeth shall prosper." – Psalm 1:3

"In the midst of the street of it, and on either side of the river, was there the tree of life, which bare twelve manner of fruits, and yielded her fruit every month: and the leaves of the tree were for the healing of the nations." – Revelation 22:2

Fruit bearing and fruitfulness are the mandate of the kingdom. Every kingdom citizen must demonstrate harvest of souls, bearing spiritual fruits and being fruitful in every good work in the kingdom. If you are truly faithful, you will be fruitful for God. Your life and ministry must be fruitful in the harvest of souls for Him, trained disciples, raised ministers and transformed destinies in the community.

By your preaching, prayers, intercessions, giving and outreaches, there must be harvest of souls into the kingdom. Your ministry must bring harvest to His kingdom. Your gifts must extent the frontiers of His kingdom into every nook and crannies of the world, where God placed you.

The Harvest Today

As our Lord Jesus says in John chapter 4 verses 35, the harvest of the world is ripe today. We are actually living in harvest time. We must each throw in our sickle to reap the harvest, else it will be lost.

God has given the sickle of time, talents and treasures to each and everyone of us.

> *"Put ye in the sickle, for the harvest is ripe: come, get you down; for the press is full, the fats overflow; for their wickedness is great."* – Joel 3:13

Harvest time doesn't last forever. All hands must therefore be on deck; else the ripened harvest will be lost forever. The following are evidences of ripened harvest today:

* He doesn't want anyone to perish – 1 Timothy 2:4
* There is openness to the gospel like never before.
* Persecution and killing of Christians is rising like never before.

* The resources to preach the gospel and disciple people are in the church.
* Many hitherto unreached places have opened up through technologies.
* Much more people are living in our cities like never before.
* Modern cults and demonic ideas of men are growing.
* 60% of world population is youths who are seeking and searching.

The reality of the ripened harvest must force us to wake up from our slumber (Proverbs 10:5), because your success during harvest is not measured by how many you have harvested, but by how many remained to be harvested. Therefore, we must all hasten to the ripened harvest fields of the world.

There are millions of billions of souls today that are yet to make intelligent decision to follow Christ whole-heartedly, and until we reach them with the true gospel so that they can accept or reject Christ, their blood will be in our hands.

> *"If thou forbear to deliver them that are drawn unto death, and those that are ready to be slain; If thou sayest, Behold, we knew it not; doth not he that pondereth the heart consider it? and he that keepeth thy soul, doth not he know it? and shall not he render to every man according to his works?"* – Proverbs 24:11-12

> *"Son of man, I have made thee a watchman unto the house of Israel: therefore hear the word at my mouth, and give them warning from me. When I say unto the wicked, Thou shalt surely die; and thou givest him not warning, nor speakest to warn the wicked from his wicked way, to save his life; the same wicked man shall die in his iniquity; but his blood will I require at thine hand. Yet if thou warn the wicked, and he turn not from his wickedness, nor from his wicked way, he shall die in his iniquity; but thou hast delivered thy soul. Again, When a righteous man doth turn from his righteousness, and commit iniquity, and I lay a stumblingblock before him, he shall die: because thou hast not given him warning, he shall die in his sin, and his righteousness which he hath done shall not be remembered; but his blood will I require at thine hand." –*
> Ezekiel 3:17-20

In the kingdom of God, there is nothing like barrenness or fruitlessness. Every kingdom citizen must bear fruit. The King of the kingdom hates barrenness.

> *"He spake also this parable; A certain man had a fig tree planted in*

> *his vineyard; and he came and sought fruit thereon, and found none. Then said he unto the dresser of his vineyard, Behold, these three years I come seeking fruit on this fig tree, and find none: cut it down; why cumbereth it the ground? And he answering said unto him, Lord, let it alone this year also, till I shall dig about it, and dung it: And if it bear fruit, well: and if not, then after that thou shalt cut it down."* – Luke 13:6-9

Barrenness or fruitlessness is a big curse in His kingdom.

> *"And on the morrow, when they were come from Bethany, he was hungry: And seeing a fig tree afar off having leaves, he came, if haply he might find any thing thereon: and when he came to it, he found nothing but leaves; for the time of figs was not yet. And Jesus answered and said unto it, No man eat fruit of thee hereafter for ever. And his disciples heard it."* – Mark 11:12-14

Therefore, you must remove all that seeks to make you barren in life and ministry for Him.

The purpose of God in calling you into His kingdom and giving gifts and ministry to you is so that you will reap the kingdom harvest for Him. And to do that you must see the vision of the harvest fields; discover the harvest He has sent you to reap; pray intensively about reaping the harvest; strategize your efforts and outreaches; use the right equipments and tools; preach the kingdom gospel wholistically; teach, train and disciple others to maturity; discover the gifts and ministries of others; mobilize and release disciples to go and harvest others and support and strengthen those who are in the harvest fields.

Your harvest here will surely be your harvest in His eternal kingdom. When He comes to harvest the world, your harvest will surely be recognized.

> *"And another angel came out of the temple, crying with a loud voice to him that sat on the cloud, Thrust in thy sickle, and reap: for the time is come for thee to reap; for the harvest of the earth is ripe."* - Revelation 14:15

> *"And they that be wise shall shine as the brightness of the firmament; and they that turn many to righteousness as the stars for ever and ever."* - Daniel 12:3

CHAPTER NINETEEN

Chapter Twenty
KINGDOM LEADERS

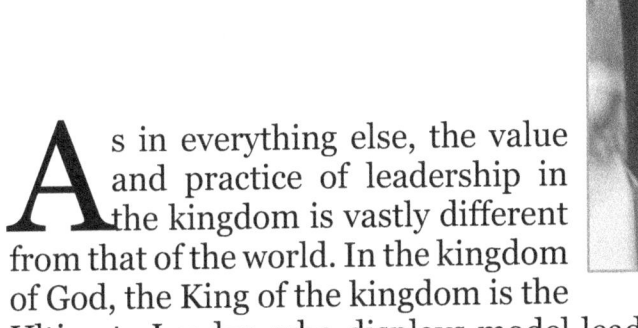

As in everything else, the value and practice of leadership in the kingdom is vastly different from that of the world. In the kingdom of God, the King of the kingdom is the Ultimate Leader, who displays model leadership in every strata. Leadership in the kingdom is by God's appointment, not human selection and a leader for God must be the true servant of all.

> *"But Jesus called them unto him, and said, Ye know that the princes of the Gentiles exercise dominion over them, and they that are great exercise authority upon them. But it shall not be so among you: but whosoever will be great among you, let him be your minister; And whosoever will be chief among you, let him be your servant: Even as the Son of man came not to be ministered unto, but to minister, and to give his life a ransom for*

many." – Matthew 20:25-28

In the Gentile kingdom, leadership is by maneuvering, domination, subjugation and oppressive tendencies, but in the kingdom, leaders and leadership is servant-hood.

A true kingdom leader is a servant; serving God by serving the people. A kingdom leader is primarily there to serve, not to be served. A true kingdom leader is not there to line his pocket, increase his fame and fortune to the detriment of God's work. Rather he sacrifices his time, talent and treasures to increase the kingdom. It is possible to be a church leader without being a kingdom leader. Church leaders need to grow up to become kingdom leaders.

Kingdom leaders are spiritual giants who undergird their leadership by the strength of their spiritual life. They are not secular and carnal but spiritually inclined persons.

Positions, titles, degrees and hierarchies don't figure in true leadership of the kingdom. True kingdom leaders are not position conscious and title wielding persons.

Leadership In The Kingdom

In the kingdom of God, leadership is not about class, status, wealth and worth, but about spiritual impact and fulfilling God's mandate. Kingdom leadership is principally spiritual. Carnal men and secular tendencies hold no value in this sphere. Kingdom leaders are those who know God, have power with Him and can subdue kingdoms in His name and power. Kingdom leaders take territories of hearts, communities and nations for God. They have vision to take whole cities and nations for God, not just content with the four walls of a local church. Kingdom leaders are those who;

> *"Through faith subdued kingdoms, wrought righteousness, obtained promises, stopped the mouth of lions, quench the violence of fire, escape the edge of the sword"* – Hebrews 11:33-34.

Traits of Kingdom Leaders

a. Kingdom leaders have massive fruits of the Spirit in their lives. Their Godly characters undergird their spiritual leadership.

b. Kingdom leaders are full of the Holy Spirit, who is the Eternal Spirit of the kingdom. Their dependence and partnership with the Holy Spirit helps them to advance the kingdom.

c. Kingdom leaders see the vision of the whole world as a mission field, not just their local church.

d. Kingdom leaders nurture and release emerging leaders to go and harvest souls into the kingdom. They influence others positively for mighty kingdom expansion.

f. Kingdom leaders don't see their local church as the kingdom of God, rather they recognize the gift and graces of God in others and encourage them to thrive for the kingdom.

g. Kingdom leaders invest in expanding the frontiers of God's kingdom into every territory, not just local cultures. They want the will of the Lord to be done in all the earth, not just within the four walls of a local church.

h. Kingdom leaders shepherd whole communities, not just their local churches. They see the communities as places that the kingdom of God must come into and works towards its actualization.

i. Kingdom leaders turn the world right side up, not just impacting local churches.

"Now when they had passed through Amphipolis and Apollonia, they came to Thessalonica, where was a synagogue of the Jews: And Paul, as his manner was, went in unto them, and three sabbath days reasoned with them out of the scriptures, Opening and alleging, that Christ

must needs have suffered, and risen again from the dead; and that this Jesus, whom I preach unto you, is Christ. And some of them believed, and consorted with Paul and Silas; and of the devout Greeks a great multitude, and of the chief women not a few. But the Jews which believed not, moved with envy, took unto them certain lewd fellows of the baser sort, and gathered a company, and set all the city on an uproar, and assaulted the house of Jason, and sought to bring them out to the people. And when they found them not, they drew Jason and certain brethren unto the rulers of the city, crying, These that have turned the world upside down are come hither also; Whom Jason hath received: and these all do contrary to the decrees of Caesar, saying that there is another king, one Jesus." - Acts 17:1-7

They seek to enthrone the rule and reign of Christ into every heart in the communities. They pray for the will of God to be done on earth as it is in heaven.

j. Kingdom leaders are competent, credible and impactful leaders who through risk-taking and forward thinking affect generations for God. They become the repairer of the breach and lay

CHAPTER TWENTY

the foundation of many generations. Are you a kingdom or local church leader?

Chapter Twenty-One
KINGDOM FINANCE

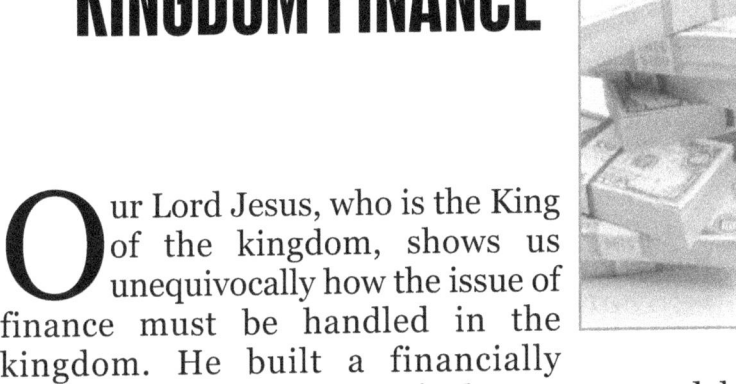

Our Lord Jesus, who is the King of the kingdom, shows us unequivocally how the issue of finance must be handled in the kingdom. He built a financially credible ministry and never had a money scandal in His work. His ministry did not suffer as a result of financial lack. He had a Treasurer that kept and disbursed the finances as the Lord gave instructions.

"Then saith one of his disciples, Judas Iscariot, Simon's son, which should betray him, Why was not this ointment sold for three hundred pence, and given to the poor? This he said, not that he cared for the poor; but because he was a thief, and had the bag, and bare what was put therein." – John 12:4-6

"And after the sop Satan entered into him. Then said Jesus unto him,

CHAPTER TWENTY-ONE

> *That thou doest, do quickly. Now no man at the table knew for what intent he spake this unto him. For some of them thought, because Judas had the bag, that Jesus had said unto him, Buy those things that we have need of against the feast; or, that he should give something to the poor."* – John 13:27-29

He depended on gifts and supports from well-meaning people whose hearts He had touched.

> *"And certain women, which had been healed of evil spirits and infirmities, Mary called Magdalene, out of whom went seven devils, And Joanna the wife of Chuza Herod's steward, and Susanna, and many others, which ministered unto him of their substance."* – Luke 8:2-3.

There were supernatural provisions too. He taught His disciples to make money for ministry work as well.

> *"Then said he unto them, But now, he that hath a purse, let him take it, and likewise his scrip: and he that hath no sword, let him sell his garment, and buy one."* – Luke 22:36

In the kingdom, it is mandatory that we get our money attitudes right, first and foremost. Even though the kingdom work demands for adequate finance, yet we are not in the kingdom for money, gain and profit. Kingdom work must never be done with the motive of money. Money must ever be a servant in the kingdom. Kingdom citizens must be free from wrong attitudes to money that is ruining the people of the world fast.

Money Personalities

In my study and research about ministers, I have come to discover the following money personalities:

a. **Taker Personality** – They just love to take, receive and not wanting to give. They believe that they are born to receive from others and never giving.

b. **Debt Personality** - They love to borrow and do things in debt and by debt. They will refuse to pay back and just like to borrow here and there.

c. **Stingy Personality** – They are too tightfisted and money-pinching. They find it difficult to release money from their pockets and hate to give to others.

d. **Covetous Personality** - Always wanting what others have, never satisfied with what God has done. They are almost always discontented.

e. **Avarice Personality** - Cheating and defrauding others to gain more. They are ready to maim, kill and destroy because of money. They love to cut corners and short-change others anyway.

f. **Spendrift Personality** - Always in the habit of buying one thing or the other. Spending and buying non-essentials.

Kingdom citizens and ministers must jettison these wrong money personalities from their lives. Kingdom citizens and ministers must be financially pure, upright and transparent. Wrong attitudes to money that manifests in these wrong money personalities must never be in the heart and life of citizens of the kingdom.

A motivational preacher said recently that there is no unclean money, and if there is any and brought to him, he will cleanse it and use it for his ministry. Well, the truth is that there is blood money and the kingdom doesn't need such monies, irrespective of what any preacher may say.

Blood Money

The kingdom of God doesn't need tainted, unclean, stolen and crooked money to thrive and expand in the world. Blood money must never be received by citizens or leaders of the kingdom.

Blood money is money gotten from hired assassins, murderers, stealing, armed or pen robbers, prostitutes, cultists, 419ers and yahoo-yahoo boys. Such monies must never be allowed into the treasury of God. That was the case with Judas Iscariot. The blood money he returned to the Priests in the temple was taken out to buy burial ground for strangers; it was never put into the treasury.

> *"Then Judas, which had betrayed him, when he saw that he was condemned, repented himself, and brought again the thirty pieces of silver to the chief priests and elders, Saying, I have sinned in that I have betrayed the innocent blood. And they said, What is that to us? see thou to that. And he cast down the pieces of silver in the temple, and departed, and went and hanged himself. And the chief priests took the silver pieces, and said, It is not lawful for to put them into the treasury, because it is the price of blood. And they took counsel, and bought with them the potter's field, to bury strangers in. Wherefore that field was called, The field of blood, unto this day."* – Matthew 27:3-8.

If religious Priests of those days could do this, how much more those of us who are ministers of a heavenly and eternal kingdom?

CHAPTER TWENTY-ONE

Money In The Kingdom

The classic scriptural passage that summarizes how finance must be handled in the kingdom is 1 Timothy chapter 6 verses 17 to 19;

> *"Charge them that are rich in this world, that they be not highminded, nor trust in uncertain riches, but in the living God, who giveth us richly all things to enjoy; That they do good, that they be rich in good works, ready to distribute, willing to communicate; Laying up in store for themselves a good foundation against the time to come, that they may lay hold on eternal life".*

Here we can deduce kingdom financial principles that will help us to handle money judiciously.

1. **It is not a crime to be financially okay.** God's blessing over your legitimate work can lead to financial buoyancy.

2. **Money must never make us to be proud, cocky or high minded.** Humility and level headedness are the marks of kingdom citizenship.

3. **Our trust must never be in money but in the Lord.** Kingdom citizens must trust in the Lord to provide, not in money. We must never

pursue money to the detriment of our faith, but to attract money through our work, products and services.

4. **It is God that richly blesses His own whichever way He chooses.** He can make all grace to abound and increase our riches.

5. **Use money to do good to others.** Money must be used to bless, edify, promote, meet needs and solve the problems of others, not to keep it for ourselves only.

6. **Giving has immediate and eternal dividends.** The more money is released upward and outward, the more God blesses now and in eternity. Money is never meant to be kept for one person alone; it must be circulated round to assist others.

The more we give away money and are honest the way we make, manage and multiply money, the more we are free from the grip and worship of money. And that is the strongest prove that we are citizens of a Godly kingdom.

CHAPTER TWENTY-ONE

Chapter Twenty-Two
KINGDOM FAMILY

God is a God of family. He hates loneliness and therefore creates family and put people in families.

"God setteth the solitary in families: he bringeth out those which are bound with chains: but the rebellious dwell in a dry land." – Psalm 68:6

"And the LORD God said, It is not good that the man should be alone; I will make him an help meet for him. And Adam said, This is now bone of my bones, and flesh of my flesh: she shall be called Woman, because she was taken out of Man. Therefore shall a man leave his father and his mother, and shall cleave unto his wife: and they shall be one flesh. And they were both naked, the man and

his wife, and were not ashamed." – Genesis 2:18, 23-25.

He desires to have a family of His own out of the whole human race. Already, He has a family in heaven (Ephesians 3:14-15) and He is still working in the world through His mighty Spirit to bring many into His family.

The eternal purpose of God is to have His creatures into one big family of His, but sin and rebellion of the human race will not allow that. So God started the process and eternal plan of salvation, that those who accept Him, repent genuinely and choose to worship Him through His Son (Genesis 3:15) will become members of His family, here and in His eternal kingdom.

God Instituted Family

God loves family and therefore places everyone in a family. He created us to be family oriented. Nobody chose his or her family, it was a divine choice. Your family has a great role to play in your life. Therefore we must all honour and cherish family. God placed the man as husband, father and head of the family, and the woman as the wife, mother and supporter. The children must obey, submit and honour their parents for the family to truly measure up to the expectation of God.

The nuclear family consisting of the father, mother and children is the perfect will of God in His word. Though there can be extended and all sorts of families, yet the nuclear one towers above all. The world is waging serious war against the family, yet people of God must build strong bulwark against the destruction of godly families in the world.

Kingdom Family

It is sad to say that not all families are kingdom family of God. The kingdom family is a home where Jesus is truly the Lord in the heart of the father and mother, plus the children. Kingdom family is where God is worshipped in spirit and truth; where the children are brought up in the fear and admonition of the Lord and the works of the devil are being daily destroyed.

Kingdom family brings glory to God by their conducts and examples and is therefore able to lead other families into the kingdom of God. Kingdom family is a model of God's love, beauty, holiness, righteousness and forbearance amidst the darkness of the world. They are shining as light and true salt in the earth. They reflect His values and are good examples of families of God.

The church is equally a kingdom family. Therefore there must be family affinity, love, acceptance, forbearance and sacrifice in each local church. We must love one another as members of God's family.

CHAPTER TWENTY-TWO

"One Lord, one faith, one baptism, One God and Father of all, who is above all, and through all, and in you all." – Ephesians 4:5-6

We must accept one another as Christ has accepted us into the glory of God. There must be no division, infighting, hatred, bitterness among and amidst the church. Carnal considerations, fleshly desires and evil practices that destroy love, justice and kindness must be put away from the church because they are marks of Satan's kingdom and not signs of the kingdom of God.

Every kingdom citizen must therefore believe in family, stay in a family, raise a kingdom family and nurture the family of God - the church. We must defend the nuclear family against the onslaught of the enemy and make sure that the family of God stays true in the world.

Chapter Twenty-Three
KINGDOM-DRIVEN MINISTER

In the kingdom, every called servant of God is a minister - we minister to God and people. Titles and positions of men do not matter; it is the heart to serve that weighs much with God.

A minister must minister to God and minister to the people. You minister to God in worship and receiving from His throne and then minister that life, fire and Zoe of God to men. It is when you are able to minister at such levels that you are truly a kingdom minister.

Of course, there are many ministers who don't minister life to people; rather they minister death, decay and destruction, simply because they have not taken time to receive from Him through their ministrations. If you don't minister to Him first, you can never minister life to the people.

CHAPTER TWENTY-THREE

Who Is A Kingdom-Driven Minister?

To be driven is to be controlled, propelled and guided by a force. A kingdom-driven minister is therefore controlled and propelled by the principles of the kingdom of God. He builds his life on seeking the kingdom in all its righteousness, becomes heavenly minded; sold out to kingdom expansion and seeks to do the perfect will of God in every area of his life.

A kingdom driven minister is in the world but the world is not in him, his values are kingdom based and do everything to expand the frontiers of God's kingdom into every nook and crannies of his world through his ministry and ministrations. A kingdom minded minister operates with these five ministry purposes:

* Builds his ministry to WORSHIP God.
* Builds his ministry to FELLOWSHIP with one another.
* Builds his ministry to EVANGELIZE.
* Builds his ministry to raise DISCIPLES for Him.
* Builds his ministry to raise MINISTERS that run their ministries.

A true kingdom minded minister will seek to build God's kingdom, not his personal empire in the hearts of men and women in the world.

The kingdom of God will outlast every other kingdom. It is in the world now, and when every other kingdom has collapsed and forgotten, it will still be around and will continue throughout eternity. What other kingdom should you work for other than this eternal kingdom?

1. Be Passionate For The Kingdom:

Reeve up your zeal and passion for His kingdom. Be sold out for the kingdom. Study, know and understand the kingdom, for that will help you to be deeply passionate for the kingdom. Your burning passion will see you promoting and doing everything for the growth and expansion of the kingdom in the world.

2. Be Kingdom-Full:

Be filled and saturated with the Spirit, grace and values of the kingdom. Let your daily life reflect the lifestyle of the kingdom. Let your life be permeated with the principles of the kingdom found in the scriptures.

> *"For the kingdom of God is not meat and drink; but righteousness, and peace, and joy in the Holy Ghost."* –
> Romans 14:17

3. Get Baptized In Kingdom Power:

The Holy Spirit is the Spirit and power of the kingdom. Seek His baptism and fresh infilling every day. Without the Spirit and power of the kingdom, you cannot be kingdom minded. Kingdom comes by power and it is the power of the Holy Spirit that will defeat the powers of the kingdom of darkness. So, get filled with the Holy Spirit and His power through fasting and prayers.

4. Preach The Gospel of The Kingdom:

You can only see and witness the kingdom in manifestation and demonstration when you preach and proclaim the gospel of the kingdom. Preaching another gospel will surely limit the advancement of His kingdom in the world.

5. Proclaim Justice In Word And Deeds

> *"He hath shewed thee, O man, what is good; and what doth the LORD require of thee, but to do justly, and to love mercy, and to walk humbly with thy God?"* – Micah 6:8

You are kingdom minded whenever you practice justice, fair play and consideration for others. Doing good works with the Spirit of Christ is real kingdom work. Taking care of the needy, fatherless, widows, downtrodden and to all are marks of His kingdom.

Showing love, concern, empathy and forbearance are all true marks of kingdom living. Denouncing cheating, dishonesty and oppression of any kind is vital to kingdom impact in the world.

Every kingdom citizen must be kingdom minded. By our works, living and choices, we must be kingdom driven. We must bring the godly values of the kingdom to our sphere of influences in the world. Our careers, jobs, ministries and families must reflect the values of His eternal kingdom. We must seek and pursue His kingdom until the knowledge of the Lord covers the earth; just as the waters cover the seas and until the kingdom of this world becomes that of Christ and God. That is His heart and His eternal desires!

CHAPTER TWENTY-THREE

Chapter Twenty-Four
KINGDOM GLORY

> *"And lead us not into temptation, but deliver us from evil: For thine is the kingdom, and the power, and the glory, for ever. Amen."* – Matthew 6:13

Jesus equates the kingdom with power and glory in this scripture. The Bible has much to say about the glory of God. The term "glory of God" is used in several ways in the scripture. It means the:

a. Splendor and majesty of God – a glory so great that no human being can look upon and live – Exodus 33:18-33.

b. Visible presence of God among His people. The Shekinah dwelling of God – Exodus 13:21; 24:16-17; 40:34-35; 1 Kings 8:11-13.

c. Spiritual presence and power of God. Christians experience God's glory and presence in His nearness, love, righteousness, and manifestations through the power of the Holy Spirit – 2 Corinthians 3:18; 1 Peter 4:14; 2 Peter 1:16-18; Acts 7:55.

1. **Jesus and The Glory of God:**

He revealed the glory of God (Isaiah 40:5; John 1:14). He had glory with the Father (John 17:5). He is the Lord of Glory (1 Cor. 2:8; James 2:1). He incarnates the glory of God and His miracles manifested His glory. (John 2:11; 11:4; Matthew 17:5).

2. **The Believer and The Glory of God:**

How does the glory of God apply to believer's individual life? Regarding God's majestic heavenly glory, no one can see it now and live (1 Timothy 6:16). However we can experience God's Shekinah Glory (Isaiah 6:1-4).

a. The Holy Spirit is the key to the spiritual manifestation of God's presence and nearness (Luke 2:8-20; 1 Corinthians 12:1-12). This is our greatest need today.

b. Kingdom glory is the mighty outworking of the Spirit in our lives and churches that demonstrate God's presence for all to see.

c. Kingdom glory is when Christians show forth the glory of God in all we do (John 17:10; 1 Cor. 10:31).

d. Kingdom glory is when the Spirit is transforming us more and more into the image of Christ (2 Cor. 3:18).

e. Kingdom glory is the visible appearance of Christ to re-assure and empower the believer while it destabilizes and destroys the enemy.

3. **Steps to Experience God's Glory**

a. Repent of sin and idols worship. Sin hinders glory.

b. Renounce all evil affinity. Evil affinity makes the glory to depart – Ezek. 10:4, 18

c. Communion with the Holy Spirit – 2 Cor. 13:14
d. Hunger and thirst for the communion with the Holy Spirit.

e. Persistent prayer for communion – Exodus 33:14-19

The manifestation of kingdom glory will bring all the difference in our lives and churches. The blessings and promotions that we seek for our lives and ministry will be adequately supplied with the manifestations of God's glory. The absence and

CHAPTER TWENTY-FOUR

departure of God's glory is the beginning of ruin and destruction – 1 Samuel 4:21-22.

Let thy Kimgdom come Oh Lord!

INTERNATIONAL CHURCH GROWTH MINISTRIES

International Church Growth Ministry was founded in 1994. The vision of the ministry is to provide current and reliable Church Growth principles in African context to Leaders, Pastors and Ministers that will lead to better and faster growth of their churches.

We do these through books, materials, VCD and audio cassettes at relatively low cost to people engaged in leading the church.

We equally organise seminars and conferences on various aspect of Church Growth and Health. We also accept invitations from churches to help analyse them, motivate their people and generally help the growth potentials of churches.

So far we have ministered to over 20,000 Pastors and Christian Workers across many denominational lines and independent churches. The results have been tremendous and the testimonies have been wonderful and interesting.

The ministry also saw the need to really raise the growth consciousness in the Continent and decided to pioneer an Institute on Church Growth. The response has been overwhelming as so many Pastors, General Overseers, and Church Leaders have enrolled to learn more about how to practically lead their churches to growth. The impact of the Institute on these Pastors' lives have started manifesting in the phenomenal growth of their churches and expansion of their ministries.

ICGM RESOURCES

If you found this book to be useful, you may be interested in some of the other books and resources produced by ICGM. Listed below are:

THE BOOKS:
1. How To Support And Strengthen Your Pastors
2. Pulpit Power For Church Growth
3. Your Growth Is Your Future
4. The Secrets Of Financially Strong Churches
5. Closing The Back Door Of Your Churches
6. Spiritual Warfare And Church Growth
7. 120 Strategic Ways To Increase Church Attendance
8. Supernatural Power, Miracles, Signs & Wonders Today
9. Our Churches And His Church
10. Strategic Living
11. Leading Your Church To Lasting Growth
12. 22 Dynamic Laws Of Church Growth
13. Strategic Church Planting Today

RESOURCES

14. The Place Of Anointing And Administration
15. The Impact Driven Church
16. Grow The Pastor, Grow The Church
17. Personal Growth Today
18. The Loyal Associate
19. Fruitful And Fulfilling Ministry Today
20. Sexual Purity In Leadership
21. Guest Ministers Today
22. Church Change
23. 25 Pillars Of Church Health
24. Quality And Quantity Growth In Churches
25. Healthy Leaders, Healthy Churches
26. Anointing Alone Is Not Enough
27. Money, Ministers & Ministry Today
28. 101 Ministry Lessons
29. Braking The Barriers Of Small, Middle-size & Mega Churches
30. Healthy Homes
31. How To Follow Well
32. The Rise & Fall Of Churches / Ministries
33. True Success, Wealth And Prosperity In Life And Ministry
34. Pray & Grow
35. 25 Indispensable Qualities of Competent And Credible Minister
36. Your Church, Your Community
37. Church Growth Principles Of Jesus
38. The Matured Pastor's Wife & Female Minister
39. Frank Talk To Men
40. The Real Man In Every Church
41. Daily Nourishment for Leaders
42. 101 Ways To Progressively Kill A Church
43. Prophets & Prophetic Ministry Today
44. Five-Fold Ministry Today

RESOURCES

45. Fundamental Teachings & Doctrines Of The Bible
46. Handling Conflict & Crisis In Ministry
47. Your Image Is Your Growth
48. Short course On Family Growth
49. Short course On Financial Growth
50. Short course On Church Growth
51. Short course On Wholesome Sexuality
52. Short course On Personal Growth

TEACHING RESOURCES:
1. Spiritual Warfare For Church Growth
2. Helping The Clergy - Leading Your Church To Growth.
3. Practical Church Planting
4. Winning The Society Seminar
5. Mobilizing The Laity
6. Warfare Prayer For Growth
7. Closing The Backdoor Of The Church
8. Women Ministry In Church Growth
9. Strategic Level Prayer For Breakthrough
10. Signs And Wonders For Church Growth
11. Research And Analysing Of The Church
12. How To Grow A Vibrant And Healthy Churches
13. Secret Of Effective & Extra-ordinary Impact Of The End Time Church
14. Causes & Cure Of Problems That Kill Churches & Ministries
15. Magnetic, Multiplying, Marketable & Maximum Impact Millennium Minister
16. Healthy, Hill-Top, High-Octane, Holistic Habits Of 21st Century Church Leader
17. Leading The 21st Century Church

RESOURCES

18. Tools For Tremendous Ministry
19. The Minister & His Ministry
20. Why Churches Lose Members
21. Church Change
22. Healthy Home, Healthy Ministry
23. Great People, Great Churches
24. The Transformational Church & Ministry
25. Money, Ministers & Ministry In The 21st Century
26. Healthy & Effective Church Planting Today
27. Healthy Home & Wholesome Church
28. Next Level Church/ministry
29. Growing, Groaning, Going, Glowing, Giving, Goal-oriented & Glorious Church
30. Powerful, Productive, Prevailing, Pragmatic, Progressive & Purpose-driven Church
31. Skills For Higher Dimension
32. Personal, Church & Ministry Financial Freedom
33. Effective Pastors For Today
34. A Well-equipped, Competent, Matured & Healthy Pastoral Leader Of Today
35. Viable Church Planting & Healthy Church Growth
36. Great Leaders, Great Ministries
37. Empowering The Church For 21st Century
38. Secrets Of Successful Churches, Significant Ministries & Supernatural Ministers
39. Leadership Without Limitation
40. Relevant & Resourceful Ministers
41. Church Without Walls
42. Healthy Leadership For Healthy Churches
43. Tools For Tremendous And Transforming Ministry.

44. New Waves Of God's Move For End Time Harvest
45. Magnetic, Multiplying, Marketable And Maximum Impact.
46. Building A Bigger, Better And Broader Church And Many Others
47. High Impact Church In Every Community
48. Difference-making Church/ministry
49. Church Overseers Course Series
50. Church Workers Congress Series
51. Real Man Seminar Series

And many more.

AUDIO TAPES, CD, VCD & MP3
All our seminars and conferences messages.

JOURNAL:
Church Growth Journal is a quarterly teaching and news magazine that gives vital and practical information on how to grow the church.

For further information on these and other resources available, please write or contact us at our office or call the telephone lines provided in this book.

RESOURCES

BOOKS AND RESOURCES
from
Dr. Bola Akin-John

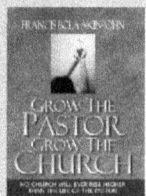

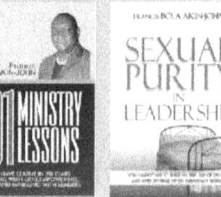

RESOURCES

   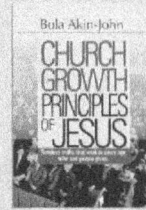 

For wholesale & retail orders, call
INTERNATIONAL CHURCH GROWTH MINISTRIES
Block C, FHA Abesan IV Estate, CF Str., off CA Str., Mosan B/Stop, Ipaja, Lagos.
Tel: +234-1-8976100, 08023000714, 08029744296
E-mail- akingrow@yahoo.com   Website: www.churchgrowthafrica.org

RESOURCES

Dr. Francis Bola AKIN-JOHN

THE AUTHOR

* Started ministry in 1988.
* Pastored five denominational churches in the space of 8 years.
* Started Church Growth Ministry in 1994 after hearing God said "Go and strengthen pastors and support churches to grow and be healthy".
* Has held hundreds of conferences across Nigeria, Africa and Europe with combined attendance of many Thousands of church leaders.
* Has written over 40 books that has sold thousands of copies.
* Founded International Institute of Church Growth that has trained over 5,000 pastors and leaders with attendant growth testimonies.
* Has written and produced hundreds of materials on various aspects of church growth, leadership and health that are being used by thousands of church leaders.
* Has mobilized and equipped men to become real men through seminars, resources and tapes.
* Has sold thousands of tapes - audio, DVD, CDs that continued to bless and edify thousands of ministers and church leaders.
* Has consulted and helped many denominational and independent churches to overcome stagnation, crisis and breakaways.
* Has been used by God to raise and grow thousands of ministers, churches and ministries across the nations.
* He is trying to live his major passion of "Empowering Leaders to Grow Healthier Churches and Ministries" across the world.

www.ingramcontent.com/pod-product-compliance
Lightning Source LLC
Chambersburg PA
CBHW031353040426
42444CB00005B/273